Caribou Inuit Traders of the Kivalliq Nunavut, Canada

Matthew Walls

BAR International Series 1895
2009

Published in 2016 by
BAR Publishing, Oxford

BAR International Series 1895

Caribou Inuit Traders of the Kivalliq Nunavut, Canada

ISBN 978 1 4073 0377 2

© M Walls and the Publisher 2009

The author's moral rights under the 1988 UK Copyright,
Designs and Patents Act are hereby expressly asserted.

All rights reserved. No part of this work may be copied, reproduced, stored,
sold, distributed, scanned, saved in any form of digital format or transmitted
in any form digitally, without the written permission of the Publisher.

BAR Publishing is the trading name of British Archaeological Reports (Oxford) Ltd.
British Archaeological Reports was first incorporated in 1974 to publish the BAR
Series, International and British. In 1992 Hadrian Books Ltd became part of the BAR
group. This volume was originally published by Archaeopress in conjunction with
British Archaeological Reports (Oxford) Ltd / Hadrian Books Ltd, the Series principal
publisher, in 2009. This present volume is published by BAR Publishing, 2016.

Printed in England

BAR titles are available from:

	BAR Publishing
	122 Banbury Rd, Oxford, OX2 7BP, UK
EMAIL	info@barpublishing.com
PHONE	+44 (0)1865 310431
FAX	+44 (0)1865 316916
	www.barpublishing.com

Preface

Abstract

In 1717 A.D., the Caribou Inuit of the Kivalliq, Nunavut were introduced to the Fur Trade through the Hudson Bay Company. It has been previously posited that between that time and 1900 A.D., the Caribou Inuit were drawn out of a traditional subsistence pattern and into an economy that was a part of a world system. However, the actual process of how trade goods and technologies were incorporated into Caribou Inuit society by the Caribou Inuit themselves has received little attention. Using a combination of archaeology, archival history, and oral history to examine the profiles of specific individuals, this report demonstrates the importance of Caribou Inuit families that acted as intermediaries between their culture and European trade in the process of Caribou Inuit economic transition during the early historic period .

Acknowledgements

This report is an adaptation of my master's thesis, which was defended at the University of Calgary, Canada in 2008. I owe my involvement in the subject matter of this study entirely to Dr. Peter C. Dawson, who first introduced me to Arctic archaeology and the Arviat Archaeology Project as an undergraduate in the summer of 2003. He devoted a large portion of the 2006 field season to the excavation of House I (see Chapter 5), encouraged my participation in the oral history side of the project, and funded my archival research in Winnipeg. My studies have benefited from his open-mindedness, originality, and support as a supervisor.

Peter Dawson at Maguse Lake, 2006

The 2006 field work at *Ihatik* would not have been possible without the help of Mr. Luke Suluk, who is Dr. Dawson's partner in the Arviat Archaeology Project. Aside from being an integral part of the excavation crew, Mr. Suluk ferried us to and from *Ihatik*, provided the use of his cabin, fed us caribou and char, and protected us from bears. I would also like to thank Mr. John Blyth and Mr. Louis Irkok who were members of the 2006 excavation crew.

2006 Excavation of House I: Louis Irkok, John Blyth, Matthew Walls, Luke Suluk.

In the summer of 2007, I had the opportunity to participate in the oral history research with the help and guidance of Dr. Natasha Lyons. It was a privilege to work with Louis Angalik, Mark Kalluak, Philip Kigusiutuak, Luke Kiniksi, and Donald Uluadluak. Their knowledge and passion for sharing history has added a unique perspective to this study.

2007 Arviat Oral History Project: Luke Kiniksi, Phillip Kigusiutuak, Louis Angalik, Donald Uluadluak, Natasha Lyons, Mark Kalluak.

At the University of Calgary, I would like to thank Dr. Gerald Oetelaar for his open-door policy, eagerness to discuss my research throughout my degree, and for being a part of my defence committee. As well, I greatly appreciate Dr. William Barr for joining my committee at the last minute, and for suggesting several critical corrections and references.

I should also mention the friends that have helped me out more than they know - especially Don Gardner, Joan Dunkley, and Latonia Hartery. Their interest in my project has been encouraging throughout my studies, and has helped me realize how lucky I am to be studying archaeology in the Canadian Arctic.

Table of Contents

PREFACE i
   ABSTRACT i
   ACKNOWLEDGEMENTS i
TABLE OF CONTENTS iii
TABLES iv
FIGURES iv
CHAPTER 1 - INTRODUCTION 1
   1.1 INTRODUCTION 1
   1.2 REPORT STRUCTURE 1
CHAPTER 2 - GEOGRAPHICAL BACKGROUND 3
   2.1 INTRODUCTION 3
   2.2 KIVALLIQ PHYSICAL GEOGRAPHY 3
   2.3 CLIMATE 3
   2.4 ANIMAL RESOURCES 4
   2.5 KIVALLIQ PREHISTORY 6
CHAPTER 3 - THE CARIBOU INUIT 9
   3.1 DEFINITION OF 'CARIBOU INUIT' 9
   3.2 MACRO-SCALE SOCIAL ORGANIZATION 9
   3.3 SUBSISTENCE AND TECHNOLOGY 9
   3.4 SOCIAL ORGANIZATION – THE FAMILY 12
   3.5 LEADERSHIP AND DECISION MAKING – THE POLITICAL PROCESS 12
   3.6 LEADERSHIP AND DECISION MAKING – THE IDEOLOGICAL BASIS 13
   3.7 CARIBOU INUIT ORIGINS AND DEVELOPMENT 13
CHAPTER 4 – CARIBOU INUIT AND THE FUR TRADE 15
   4.1 INTRODUCTION 15
   4.2 1611-1717 EARLY EXPLORATIONS OF HUDSON BAY 15
   4.4 EUROPEAN IMPACT ON CARIBOU INUIT CULTURE IN THE EARLY PERIOD OF HBC TRADE 19
   4.5 THE DEVELOPMENT OF CARIBOU INUIT/EUROPEAN RELATIONS 19
   4.6 SUMMARY OF THE EARLY PERIOD OF TRADE 1717-1790 21
   4.7 1790-1900 THE INUIT TRADERS 22
   4.8 PROFILES OF CARIBOU INUIT TRADERS 26
   4.9 DISCUSSION 31
CHAPTER 5 – ARCHAEOLOGY OF HOUSE I 33
   5.1 INTRODUCTION 33
   5.2 THE HOUSE I EXCAVATION 37
   5.3 PART 1: STRATIGRAPHY 38
   5.3 PART 2: ARTIFACTS 40
   5.3 PART 3: HOUSE I FAUNAL ANALYSIS 50
   5.3 PART 4: ARCHITECTURAL DISCUSSION 58
   5.3 PART 5: ACTIVITY AREAS 60
CHAPTER 6 – DISCUSSIONS AND CONCLUSION 63
   6.1 HOUSE I DISCUSSION 63
   6.2 CONCLUSIONS AND DIRECTIONS FOR FUTURE RESEARCH 64
BIBLIOGRAPHIC REFERENCES 67

Tables

TABLE 1 KIVALLIQ METEOROLOGICAL DATA 5
TABLE 2 KIVALLIQ BIRDS UTILIZED BY HUMANS..6
TABLE 3 KIVALLIQ FISH UTILIZED BY HUMANS 6
TABLE 4 KIVALLIQ ARCHAEOLOGICAL CULTURES 7
TABLE 5 EARLY HUDSON BAY EXPLORERS 15
TABLE 6 CONTENTS OF AN 1864 AHIARMIUT TRADE AT CHURCHILL POST 28
TABLE 7 QUANTITIES OF FEATURE TYPES AT THE *IHATIK* SITE (JHKL – 1 & 2) 33
TABLE 8 HOUSE I ARTIFACT QUANTITIES AND REPRESENTATION 49
TABLE 9 SUMMARY OF HOUSE I FAUNAL ASSEMBLAGE 51
TABLE 10 SEAL ELEMENT SUMMARY 55
TABLE 11 CARIBOU ELEMENT SUMMARY..56

Figures

FIGURE 1 GEOGRAPHICAL MAP OF THE KIVALLIQ, NUNAVUT 4
FIGURE 2 QAMANIRJUAQ HERD SEASONAL MOVEMENT 5
FIGURE 3 CARIBOU INUIT SUB-DIVISIONS 10
FIGURE 4 HUNTING BLIND AT MAGUSE LAKE 10
FIGURE 5 CARIBOU CROSSING THE MAGUSE RIVER 11
FIGURE 6 HUDSON BAY 1717-1900 A.D. 16
FIGURE 7 CENTRAL ARCTIC 25
FIGURE 8 H.H. HALL'S MAP 29
FIGURE 9 DONALD ULUADLUAK'S DRAWING OF QIQUT 30
FIGURE 10 AUSTIN ISLAND, NUNAVUT 33
FIGURE 11 MAP OF THE IHATIK SITE (JHKL 1 & 2) 34
FIGURE 12 HOUSE I PHOTOS 35
FIGURE 13 HOUSE I LOCAL TOPOGRAPHY 37
FIGURE 14 CARIBOU INUIT SUMMER TENT 38
FIGURE 15 HOUSE I SPATIAL LAYOUT AND EXCAVATION UNITS 38
FIGURE 16 STRATAGRAPHIC PROFILES, HOUSE I 39
FIGURE 17 NORTH WALL COMPOSITION 40
FIGURE 18 HOUSE I ARTIFACTS AND FAUNAL MATERIALS 41
FIGURE 19 NAILS RECOVERED FROM HOUSE I 42
FIGURE 20 METAL ARTIFACTS FROM HOUSE I 44
FIGURE 21 GROUND-SLATE ULU AND BEAD/COPPER ORNAMENT FROM HOUSE I 45
FIGURE 22 ANTLER AND BONE TOOLS FROM HOUSE I 47
FIGURE 23 PHOTO OF CACHE CONTAINING A BELUGA SPINAL COLUMN, 8M SOUTH OF HOUSE I 53
FIGURE 24 RICHARD HARRINGTON'S PHOTO OF AN AHIARMIUT TENT AT PADLEI 59
FIGURE 25 G. STEENHOVEN'S PHOTO OF AN ELONGATED AHIARMIUT TENT AT ENNADAI LAKE, 1955 59
FIGURE 26 PHOTO OF AN *IHATIK* TENT RING OF COMPARABLE DIMENSIONS TO HOUSE I 60

Chapter 1 - Introduction

1.1 Introduction

This study explores the relationship between the Caribou Inuit and the Fur Trade in the Kivalliq Barrens of Nunavut, Canada, between the years 1717-1900 A.D. It has previously been posited that with the introduction of European technologies during this period, the Caribou Inuit were drawn out of a traditional pattern of subsistence and into a larger world-scale economic system (see Burch 1986; Csonka 1994; Damas 1988; Fossett 2001; Vallee 1967; Williamson 1974). Arctic anthropologists have often used historical data, exclusively, to examine this transition – an approach which necessarily biases the examination of development to a colonial point of view, therefore removing the agency of the Inuit in the process (Cabak & Loring 2000: 2; Leone & Potter 1988; Jones 1989: 9-12). In general, a common element of such studies is that it is assumed that the Caribou Inuit pursued the new and highly functional technologies introduced by the Hudson Bay Company, such as metal implements and firearms, and by doing so were drawn into an economy of trade (Jones 1989). However, the actual process of how European goods and technologies were integrated into Caribou Inuit society, by the Caribou Inuit themselves, has received little attention, and more rarely has this process been studied beyond historical documentation through the use of archaeology.

This study seeks to rectify the situation by specifically examining Caribou Inuit individuals of the period, who were independent traders that acted as middlemen between the bulk of the Caribou Inuit population and the Hudson Bay Company. In order to create profiles of such individuals, the research strategy has drawn upon three primary sources. The first is a re-examination of historical documentation at the Hudson Bay Company Archives at the Provincial Archives of Manitoba in Winnipeg. As well, this study has drawn heavily upon the Arviat Oral History Project, which is currently in process, and has been running since 2005 (see Dawson et al. 2006; Lyons 2007). The Arviat Oral History Project is being conducted by Dr. Peter Dawson and Dr. Natasha Lyons, in conjunction with the Nunavut Department of Education and the Padlirmiut[1] Elders of Arviat, Nunavut. Finally, this study uses archaeology to examine an unusual semi-subterranean house structure which dates to this critical time period, and was occupied by a Caribou Inuit family who, I argue, were independent traders.

1.2 Report Structure

Chapters 2 and 3 provide a requisite geographical and cultural background. The environment of the Kivalliq is briefly described with an emphasis upon the distances and characteristics of the terrain, the climate and nature of seasons, and the animal resources around which traditional life was orientated. The very definition of 'Caribou Inuit' is discussed, along with the traditional patterns of subsistence and technology. The social structure and ideology of the Caribou Inuit are examined, with specific attention to the concept of leadership and decision making. Discussion of leadership and family politics is particularly important because Caribou Inuit traders can be seen as individuals who did not necessarily adhere to traditional concepts of subsistence.

Chapter 4 examines the origin and nature of the relationship between the Caribou Inuit and European trade. A large portion of Chapter 4 is devoted to a chronological depiction of major events that are apparent in historical records. It is accepted, however, that the historical approach is biased towards a European characterization of events. An attempt is made to balance this by addressing an Inuit point of view, drawing primarily upon Padlirmiut Elder knowledge from the aforementioned Arviat Oral History Project. The ultimate objective of Chapter 4, once the time period has been described, is to examine the profiles of specific Caribou Inuit individuals who were intermediaries between their culture and European trade.

In Chapter 5, I discuss the results of excavations carried out at the *Ihatik* site (JhKl – 1 & 2) on Austin Island, Nunavut during the summer of 2006 (Dawson et al. 2007). One particular structure, named 'House I' during excavation, is of interest to this study because it is highly irregular when compared to typical Caribou Inuit dwellings, and was probably occupied between 1850 - 1900 A.D. The report analyzes the artifacts, faunal materials, architecture, and location of House I. This data will be used to argue that the anomalous nature of House I is best understood in the context of how Caribou Inuit traders conducted their business in the 1800s.

House I is therefore particularly meaningful in the examination of the relationship between the Caribou Inuit and the Fur Trade. Chapter 6 discusses the archaeological conclusions drawn from House I in that context; this will include implications about the nature of the economic transition of the Caribou Inuit between 1717 and 1900 A.D. As well, Chapter 6 suggests possible directions for future research regarding the development of Caribou Inuit culture, and how the conclusions of this study are of relevance to Arctic archaeology in general.

---

[1] The Padlirmiut are a group of Caribou Inuit. A complete description of Caribou Inuit sub-groupings can be found in Chapter 3

Chapter 2 - Geographical Background

2.1 Introduction

The Caribou Inuit are native to the region lies west of Hudson Bay, now encompassed by the Kivalliq[2] district of Nunavut. Although singularly immense, and often simply referred to as 'the Barrens', the Kivalliq is a geographically diverse region with many local ecological intricacies that are unique in their own respect. This chapter briefly describes the geography of the Kivalliq. Such a depiction is necessary to understand the individuals with which this study is concerned, the conditions in which they lived, the distances they travelled, and the resources that they depended upon.

2.2 Kivalliq Physical Geography

The Caribou Inuit territory is bounded by the tree line to the South, the Back River system to the North, and the coast of Hudson Bay to the East (Figure 1). This area consists of approximately 300 000 km square of tundra, which, to give a sense of scale, would easily fit a country the size of Italy or the United Kingdom. As a part of the Canadian Shield, the base geology consists of pre-Cambrian sandstone and granite. Other than bedrock outcrops, which often form ridges and plateaus, the only other topographical features are glacial deposits that were formed during the last ice-age, including elongated drumlins, eskers, and moraines, that are all generally oriented from east to west in accordance with the movement of the Laurentide ice-sheet (Robinson 1968: 201-209).

The landscape is relatively flat with a maximum elevation of 500 m above sea level, which makes landforms such as eskers and bedrock outcrops all the more prominent (Robinson 1968: 207-209). From atop, the normal view between such landforms and the next includes countless lakes, ponds and marshes. Most of the Kivalliq is very poorly drained, resulting in a plethora of stagnant water-bodies of various sizes (Robinson 1968: 207). During the summer, patches of land are covered by lichen and moss with clusters of flowers, berries, and dwarf willows (Thompson et al. 1988: 123; Ritchie 2004: 16-17; Robinson 1968: 210; Savile 1968: 401-404). By winter, the entire landscape is covered by snow drifts (Thompson 1968: 267).

The Kivalliq is divided by several river systems which connect to Hudson Bay either directly, or through Chesterfield Inlet (Gagnon 2002; Robison 1968:207-209). These rivers, and the lakes they fill, are the primary routes of navigation and travel used by humans and animals (Gordon 1974: 7; Keith 2004). From the North, the Thelon, Dubawnt, and Kazan River systems all drain first into Baker Lake, then into Hudson Bay through Chesterfield Inlet. Other major systems, which drain directly into Hudson Bay include the Ferguson, Maguse, McConnell, Thlewiaza, Tha-Anne, and Seal Rivers (Figure 1).

South of Arviat, Hudson Bay is very shallow and has dramatic tides that do not rise to a definite coastline, but rather a massive stretch of mud flats that form a unique salt-marsh habitat (Dawson et al 2006:12; Cooch 1968: 449-450). Hudson Bay tides in general are among the most dramatic in the world, and in some areas can expose tidal flats that stretch 5 km between high and low tide (Freeman & Murty 1976). To the North of Arviat, the coastline is jagged with a number of elongated island chains, formed by eskers that stretch out into the Bay (Figure 1) (Robinson 1968: 207-210).

2.3 Climate

The weather in the Kivalliq can be volatile at all times of the year. Blizzards, fogs, high winds, and storms form quickly and can linger for weeks at a time. Winds shift frequently, usually signalling a negative change in weather. Local factors that affect the climate of the Kivalliq include Hudson Bay, the Arctic Coast to the northwest, and the interior expanse of tundra (Thompson 1968: 263-266). The Kivalliq is also affected by the regional movement of systems which generally follow a westerly pattern (Thompson 1968:265). The mean annual temperature and precipitation vary considerably throughout the region, mostly becoming colder and dryer towards the North (see Table 1).

The Arctic air mass descends on the Kivalliq in September, bringing the onset of autumn. The winter freeze-up of rivers usually occurs by late-October, and spring break-up by early July, but the timing of both can be highly erratic from one year to the next (Thompson 1968: 265-280). The total number of frost-free days rarely exceeds 90, resulting in a very short growing season (Macpherson 1968: 472; Robinson 1968:311)

Precipitation overall is fairly low, between 20-30 centimetres a year, and occurs mostly in June and October (Burch 1986: 108; Zoltai & Johnson 1978: 7-8). Heavy rains, which sometimes occur late in the fall, can quickly freeze preventing animals from eating the vegetation below during the winter (Thompson 1968:269). Such climatic events can have significant consequences that impede travel and cause resource shortages. Migrations of animals have definite patterns and routes, yet they can be randomly disrupted by early frost or premature river break-ups (Macpherson 1968: 475-476). Though the changes in season are inevitable, their transitions are temperamental and variable between years; the climate of the Kivalliq is highly unpredictable.

---

[2] Although the current district boundary of the Kivalliq includes Southampton Island and Repulse Bay, these areas are beyond the native territory of the Caribou Inuit, and are not included by the term 'Kivalliq' when used in this report (see Figure 7).

Figure 1 Geographical Map of the Kivalliq, Nunavut

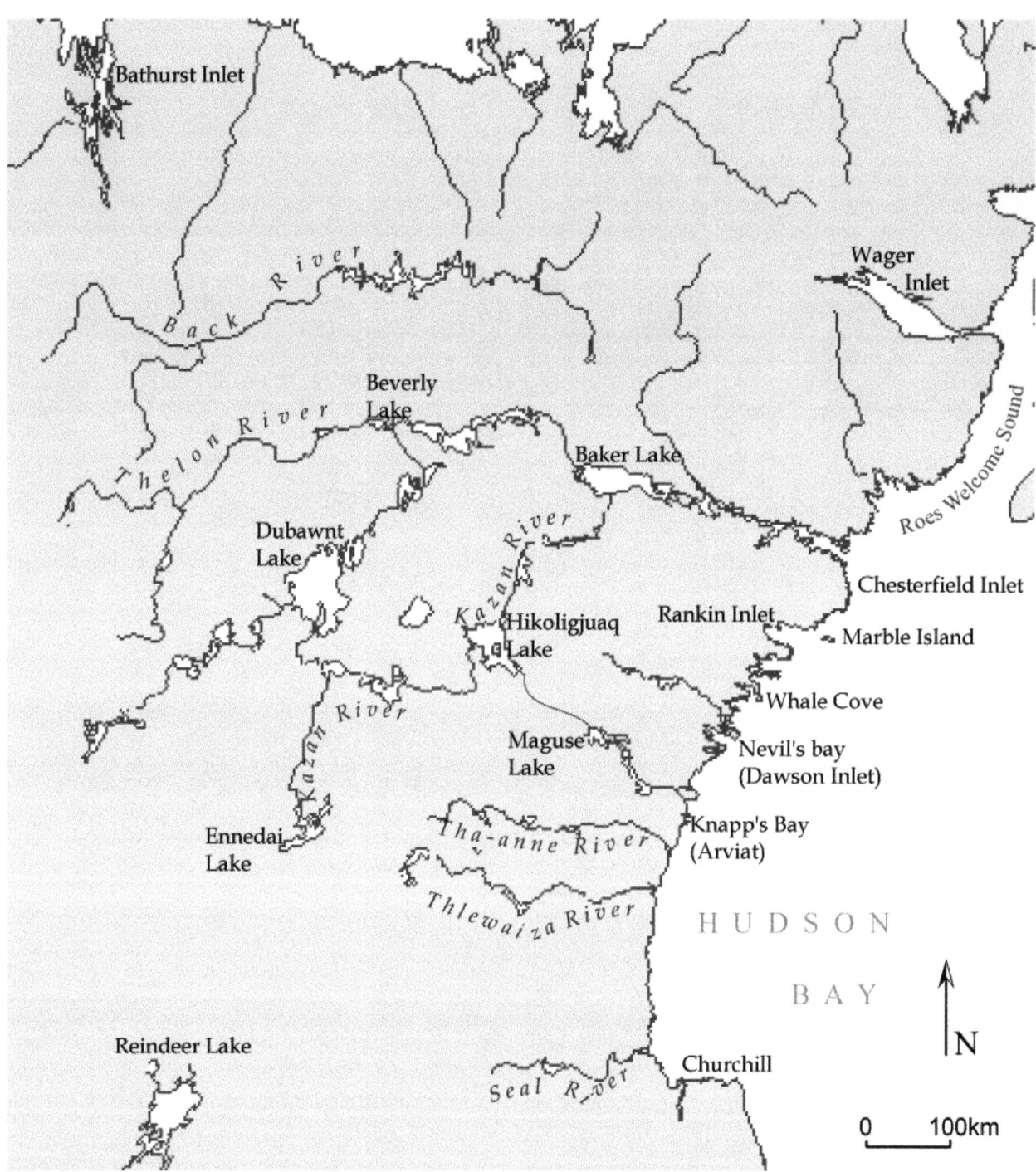

2.4 Animal Resources

Caribou (Rangifer tarandus)

In the summer, the landscape of the Kivalliq is anything but the desolate image conjured by the term 'barren'. On the contrary, the tundra is said, by the Inuit, to rumble and vibrate with the sound of caribou hoofs as they migrate to and from the calving grounds around Qamanirjuaq Lake in the spring and fall (Figure 2) (Rasmussen 1930: 40). The Qamanirjuaq herd, native to the Kivalliq, currently includes approximately 500 000 animals, but probably had a larger population at normal times in prehistory (Wakelyn 1999:3). In June, females start to show up on the tundra, slowly making their way to the calving grounds (Gates 1989: 125; Macpherson 1968: 481-483; Riewe 1992: 191). They are usually in poor health after the winter, and travel in small groups which are easily scared and hard to catch off-guard. After calving in July, they are joined by the males, and the herds grow very large. During the early summer, they are

Table 1 Kivalliq Meteorological Data (Zoltai & Johnson 1978:7)

Meteorological Station	Mean Total Precipitation	Number of Frost-Free Days	Mean Daily Temperature
Ennedai Lake (South)	286 mm	102	-9.6° C
Baker Lake (North)	213 mm	86	-12.4° C

still in poor shape, and are constantly harassed by insects; they have very little fat during this period and their hides are very thin with lots of holes created by warble larvae. By the late-summer to early-fall, they are in much better health with lots of rich fat and good quality hides. The migration back to the tree line occurs *en masse*, unlike the spring migration (Burch 1986: 121; Rasmussen 1930:42). As they migrate, their movement is bounded at times by lakes and rivers which divert the caribou to shallow river crossings. Although the migration routes do change from year to year, there are certain locations that are likely to be high-traffic areas as a result (Louie Angalik in Dawson et al 2007: 19; Arima 1984: 448-449). Other than humans, the only predators which hunt the caribou are barren-grounds grizzlies (*Ursus arctos*), polar bears (*Ursus maritimus*), and tundra wolves (*Canis lupus*) (Banfield 1974: 296).

Figure 2 Qamanirjuaq Herd Seasonal Movement

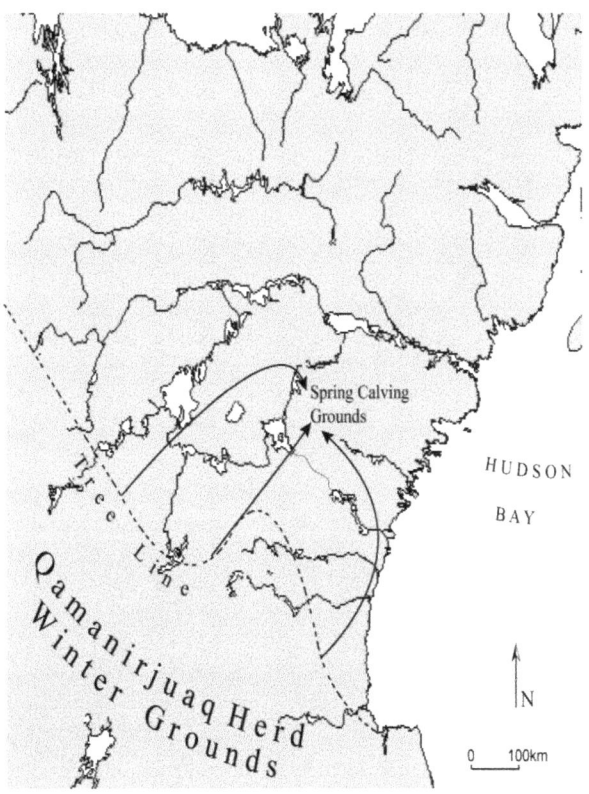

Musk-Ox

Small herds of musk-ox (*Ovibos moschatus*) also lived in the Caribou Inuit territory. They were over hunted in the 1800s, bringing them to near extinction, but in prehistory there were probably small herds of 6-12 individuals scattered throughout the Kivalliq (Barr 1991: 1; Banfield 1974: 411-414). Now that they are no longer endangered, their populations are rebounding and move further south every year (Suluk 2007: personal communication). Although they were never as numerous as the caribou, they were an important resource because they stayed on the tundra during the winter (Burch 1986: 121).

Birds

Millions of migratory birds arrive on the tundra in early spring to nest at ponds and marshes. This includes a variety of species of economic value to humans including geese, ducks, herons, loons, swans, gulls, ptarmigans, and smaller birds. During this period, families and nests of waterfowl can be found at all of the marshes and ponds. Most of the birds are not very mobile once eggs are laid, when there are hatchlings, nor during the moult (Cooch 1968: 443-450). Until they migrate South, by October, birds are easy prey for some of the smaller predators such as Arctic foxes (*Alopex lagopus*) and wolverines (*Gulo gulo*). These predators also rely on Arctic hares (*Lepus arcticus*) and other *rodentia*, such as ground squirrels (*Spermophilius undulates*) and lemmings (*Lemmus sibiricus*) once the birds have gone (Banfield 1974: 297-298, 332-334).

Fish

Fish are one of the most stable resources in the Kivalliq (Burch 1986: 121). Arctic char, an anadromous *salmonid*, are the most numerous; they spawn each year by the thousands, travelling from Hudson Bay, up the rivers and into the lakes where many spend the winter before returning to the Bay once the rivers break up in the spring. Native to the rivers and lakes themselves are many species of trout, whitefish, grayling, and pike. Even during inclement years, when the weather has been temperamental causing shortages of other resources, fish can be caught all year round (Burch 1986: 121).

Table 2 Kivalliq Birds Utilized by Humans (Birket-Smith 1929a; Gordon 1974:23-24)

Species
Ducks
Mallard (*Anas platyrhnchos*)
Pintail (*Anas acuta*)
Geese
Canada Goose (*Branta canadensis*)
Snow Goose (*Chen caerulsecens*)
White Fronted Goose (*Anser albifrons*)
Loons
Arctic loon (*Gavia arctica*)
Common loon (*Gavia immer*)
Red-throated loon (*Gavia adamsii*)
Ptarmigan
Rock ptarmigan (*Lagopus mutus*)
Willow ptarmigan (*Lagopus lagopus*)
Gulls
Arctic tern (*Sterna paradisaea*)
Herring gull (*Larus argentatus*)
Mew gull (*Larus bracyrhyncus*)
Swans
Whistling swan (*Olor columbianus*)

Table 3 Kivalliq Fish Utilized by Humans (Birket-Smith 1929a; Gordon 1974:23-24)

Species
Arctic char (*Salvelinus alpinus*)
Grayling (*Thymallus arcticus*)
Herring (*Coregonus sardinella*)
Humpback whitefish (*Coregonus clupeaformis*)
Lake trout (*Salvelinus namaycush*)
Northern pike (*Esox lucius*)
Round whitefish (*Prosopium cylinraceum*)

Sea-mammals

There are a wide variety of sea-mammals that live in Hudson Bay and are available along the coastline. Seals can be found about the estuaries of rivers where they feed. By summer, this includes Bearded and Harbour seals. The latter can occasionally be found hundreds of kilometres up the rivers and lakes as well (Banfield 1974:369-371; Mansfield 1968:382-383). Once the Bay freezes and land-fast ice has formed, Ringed and Bearded seals can be found at breathing holes close to the floe edge (Mark Kalluak in Dawson et al. 2006: 71; Lunn et al. 1997: 915; Mansfield 1968: 381; Riewe 1991: 5-6; Smith 1975: 175). Walrus are present in Hudson Bay, predominantly to the North of Whale Cove; however, prehistoric populations were present as far to the South as Churchill (see Figure 1) (Louie Angalik in Dawson et al. 2006: 10; Dawson 2005: 34; Mansfield 1968: 384-387). Beluga and Narwhal whales are also available in pods of 30-40 individuals. They feed on migratory fish moving from one estuary to another during the summer and migrate south with the edge of the ice pack during the winter (Sergeant 1968: 388-391). Bowhead whales can also be found in Hudson Bay, and although endangered at present, likely had a larger population and distribution in prehistory as well (Banfield 1974: 281; Sergeant 1968: 393).

2.5 Kivalliq Prehistory

During the historic period, the Kivalliq was simultaneously occupied by Chipewyan and Inuit peoples, but archaeological evidence suggests that human occupation of the Kivalliq extends 8000 years into prehistory as well (Table 4) (Smith & Burch 1979; Gordon 1994). The oldest archaeological sites are associated with the Northern Plano Tradition, generally dating to around 8000 B.P. The Northern Plano Tradition is characterized by large lancelet points which are stylistically similar to Agate Basin points on the Northern Plains (Gordon 1994: 219). James V. Wright and Bryan Gordon argue that the Northern Plano Tradition evolved into the Shield Archaic Tradition which occurred in the Kivalliq from 6500-3500 B.P. (Gordon 1994: 201; Wright 1976: 82). The Shield Archaic is characterized by smaller side-notched and corner-notched points, often similar to Oxbow, Duncan, and McKean type points of the Northern Plains (Gordon 1994: 201-203). Shield Archaic peoples were replaced about 3450 years ago by Pre-Dorset peoples of the Arctic Small Tool Tradition. The Pre-Dorset, although characteristically an Arctic culture, occupied sites as far to the South as Churchill, Manitoba (Nash 1972: 15). Shortly after the Pre-Dorset, around 2700 B.P., people of the Thaltheilei culture moved into the Kivalliq. The Thaltheilei culture is probably ancestral to the Dene and Chipewyan peoples that were present in the Kivalliq during the Historic period (Gordon 1994: 239). As early as 600 B.P., Thule culture peoples, who are also the ancestors of the Historic Inuit were present in the Kivalliq (Gordon 1988). The historic period of the Kivalliq began in 1717 A.D., with the opening of Fort Prince of Wales at Churchill, Manitoba. After this period, the Thaltheilei and Thule cultures are referred to by archaeologists using their indigenous names.

The people who lived in the Kivalliq during the last 8000 years came from a variety of geographical origins including the Arctic, Boreal Forest, and the Plains, yet all seem to have been drawn to the Kivalliq for the same reason – the caribou. The hundreds of thousands of caribou, of the Qamanirjuaq herd, provided for nearly

Table 4 Kivalliq Archaeological Cultures

Archaeological Culture	Approximate Dates³	Geographical Origin	Key References
Northern Plano Tradition	8000-7000 B.P.	Plains	Wright 1976; Gordon 1974
Shield Archaic	6500-3500 B.P.	Plains	Wright 1972; Harp 1961
Pre-Dorset	3450-2650 B.P.	Arctic	Nash 1972
Thaltheilei	2700-300 B.P.	Boreal Forest	Gordon 1996
Thule	600-300 B.P.	Arctic	Gordon 1988
Chipewyan	Unknown – 1790 A.D.	Boreal Forest	Hearne 1958
Caribou Inuit	Unknown – Present	Arctic	Birket-Smith 1929a; Burch 1986

all of the subsistence needs of humans in the Kivalliq for the last 8000 years (Gordon 1974). As a result, people were subject to the ecology and annual migrations of the caribou herds, and the climatic events which affected their movement. The technological differences between the archaeological cultures that have been discussed are beyond the scope of this study. However, it should be noted that what these cultures have in common is a high degree of mobility and pattern of subsistence that matched the annual movement of the caribou (Gordon 1994; 1974).

---

³ Dates measured 'B.P.' (Before Present) represent radiocarbon sources. Dates acquired from historical sources are represented according to the Julian Calendar.

Chapter 3 - The Caribou Inuit

3.1 Definition of 'Caribou Inuit'

'Caribou Eskimo' is a term that was coined by Knud Rasmussen (1930) and Kaj Birket-Smith (1929a)[4] to define the Inuit living in the Kivalliq territory. Although there was no political grounding to define the Caribou Inuit as a consolidated entity, the term is still used by anthropologists because it accurately delineates the fact that most of the Inuit living in this region have a very unique way of life when compared to the neighbouring Aivilingmiut, Copper Inuit, and Netsilik, or indeed most other Inuit groups across the Arctic (see Figure 3). In contrast to the Inuit archetypal reliance on sea-mammals for subsistence, the Caribou Inuit emphasized terrestrial resources, most notably the caribou of the Qamanirjuaq herd. Along with the overwhelming importance of the caribou, the Caribou Inuit have a common linguistic heritage, which also separates them from other Central Inuit groups to the North and West (Arima 1984: 447; Burch 1978: 20, 1986: 107; Dorais 1990: 83, 85-86; Keith 2004: 41; Williamson 1974: 17-19). Externally, other Inuit groups referred to the Caribou Inuit by collective names. For example, Copper Inuit and Iglulingmiut respectively referred to the Caribou Inuit as the *Palliq* and the *Agutit* (see Arima 1984: 462; Boas 1889: 42-43; Jenness 1922).

3.2 Macro-scale Social Organization

The Caribou Inuit, who probably numbered no more than 2000 at any one point in time before 1950, are usually divided into five main groups: Ahiarmiut, Harvaqtormiut, Hauniqturmiut, Padlirmiut, and Qairnirmiut (Figure 3) (Burch 1986:109). The definition of these groups has always been problematic for anthropologists because the divisions have little political meaning and their definitions are highly ephemeral. In the case of the Padlirmiut for example, there are many more subdivisions to which people claim membership, often identifying themselves as 'Padlirmiut' in one context, but by other names once the context changes. Consider this quote provided by Geert van den Steenhoven:

> "...when I am in Padlermiut territory, I am a Padlermiut, but if I go to Padley (which is still located in Padlermiut territory), then I become an Ahearmiut... those at Ennadai Lake claim that they are Ahearmiut and NOT Padlermiut. But the Eskimos at Yathkyed Lake[5] call themselves Padlermiut, and never Ahearmiut." – (Steenhoven 1955a: 46)

Burch describes the five groups as societies that are a distinct set of families connected to one another by marriage and kinship, and are attached to defined territories (Burch 1986:115-116). It would seem however, that there was a great deal of intermarriage between the different groups. Rasmussen reported that as many as a quarter of all marriages were exogamous (Arima 1984: 454; Rasmussen 1930: 11-13, 22-23). For example, of the three Padlirmiut Elders participating in the Arviat Oral History Project, all have at least one parent from another group (Dawson et al. 2006: 6-7, 101). Territory does not seem to have been a defining factor either as it was common for individuals to change locations many times during the course of their lives, often living in territories that would normally be associated with another group (Louie Angalik & Mark Kalluak in Dawson et al 2006: 13, 15; Rasmussen 1930: 8). R.G. Williamson points out that generically, circumpolar Inuit have little tendency towards "ethnic-group loyalty", as the basic social and political unit is the extended family (Williamson 1974: 31).

Even so, some generalizations about territory and group subsistence can be made (Figure 3). The Ahiarmiut and Harvaqtormiut would spend the entire year inland, and relied almost exclusively upon caribou. Both groups were mostly attached to the Kazan River system with Hikoligjuaq Lake as the dividing line (Harper 1964; Keith 2004). The Qairnirmiut and Hauniqturmiut both spent the early summers on the coast hunting seals and beluga, but would travel inland by August, remaining there for the winter (Burch 1986: 115-116; Rasmussen 1930: 10-11). The Padlirmiut, who were the largest of the five groups by 1922, seem to have adopted both strategies. Many Padlirmiut spent the entire year inland, and were also associated with Hikoligjuaq Lake and the Kazan River system. Other Padlirmiut would travel down the Maguse River into Maguse Lake, and at least some would spend the late spring and early summers on the coast, meeting at large aggregation sites to hunt sea-mammals (Birket-Smith 1929a: 130-132, 134-136).

3.3 Subsistence and Technology

The caribou provided for most of the needs of the Caribou Inuit from food, to clothing, shelter, and tools (Arima 1984: 448; Burch 1986: 120). As a result, the subsistence patterns and technologies of the Caribou Inuit are reflective of this dependence; indeed, the very pulse and pattern of traditional life revolved around the seasonal movements and behaviours of the Qamanirjuaq herd.

Before the introduction of the gun, the spring and summer were often sparse periods (Rasmussen 1930:41-42). During these seasons, the Inuit would herd groups of caribou using drive lanes constructed with stone cairns (Birket-Smith 1929a: 110- 111). The drive lanes would direct caribou to locations where hunters,

---

[4] Birket-Smith and Rasmussen were the Danish ethnographers who produced the first seminal ethnography of the Caribou Inuit. They passed through the region in 1922, as a part of the Danish Fifth Thule Expedition, with the purpose of exploring and mapping the Inuit cultures of the Arctic.

[5] Yathkyed Lake is referred to as Hikoligjuaq Lake in this report for continuity with the majority of ethnographic and oral-history sources.

Figure 3 Caribou Inuit Sub-Divisions

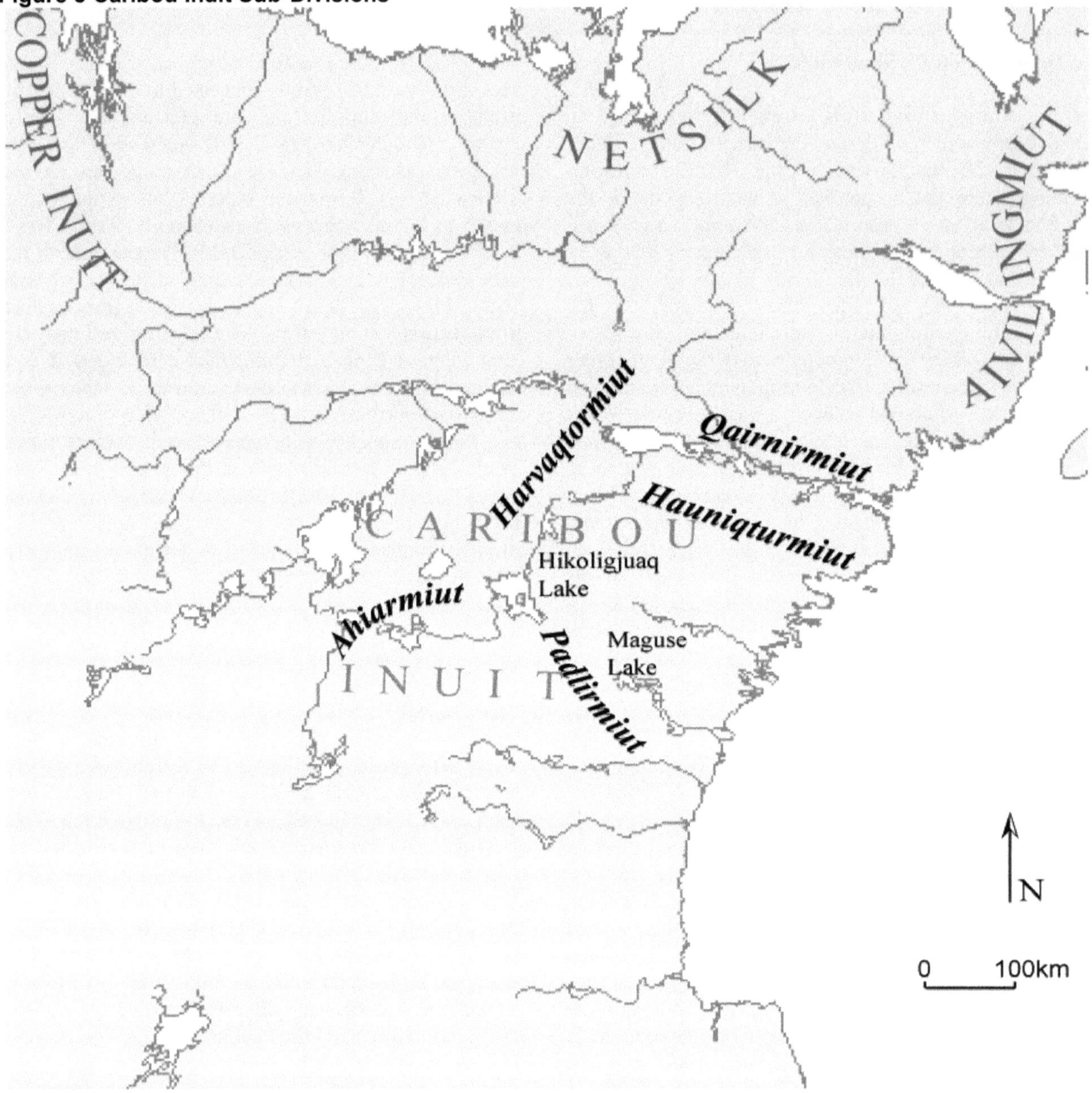

who were hidden behind hunting blinds, would kill them using lances or the bow and arrow (Figure 4) (Louie Angalik in Dawson et al. 2006: 21-22; Lyons 2007:13; Rasmussen 1930: 40). Other strategies that were sometimes used were less successful, but included chasing the caribou on foot, or trapping them in snow pits (Rasmussen 1930: 41-42). Because of the leanness and paucity of meat on the caribou, they were usually hunted for immediate consumption and day-to-day needs during this period (Louie Angalik in Dawson et al. 2006: 18; Burch 1986: 121).

The main caribou hunt occurred from late-August to October (Louie Angalik in Dawson et al. 2006: 18-20; Burch 1986:121). Towards the middle of August, when the caribou are at their strongest, their numbers give them a sense of security and it was easy for the Caribou Inuit to kill large numbers of them (Harper 1964:

Figure 4 Hunting Blind at Maguse Lake

10-14). The most common strategy was to ambush the caribou with kayaks as they crossed rivers. The caribou, once committed to crossing, were helpless and could simply be killed from kayaks with lances (Figure 5) (Arima 1975: 147-153). This made caribou crossings significant locations, and Inuit camps were usually in close proximity throughout the fall (Louie Angalik in Dawson et al. 2006: 20; Bennett & Rowley 2004: 64; Harper 1964: 13). The caribou hunt was constant during this period, and any breaks were spent preparing hides and storing meat for the winter. Fall was the single most important time of the year because it provided almost all of the food to be eaten for the winter (Bennett & Rowley 2004: 63-4, 245-249; Birket Smith 1929a: 110-111; Burch 1986: 120-121; Friesen & Stewart 2004: 35; Rasmussen 1930: 42-43).

Figure 5 Caribou Crossing the Maguse River

(Photo credit: Peter Dawson)

Once winter begins in the Kivalliq, there is very little food in the interior. Occasionally, Qamanirjuaq stragglers get trapped on the tundra and can be hunted, but never with the same success as during the fall (Rasmussen 1930:27). Musk-ox, which are non-migratory, were available throughout the winter in much smaller quantities than the caribou. The normal technique used by the Caribou Inuit was to use dogs to provoke the herds of 6-12 animals into a defensive ring, at which point they were killed with heavy lances and arrows (Barr 1991: 1; Birket-Smith 1929a: 112). Musk-ox were not a major part of subsistence in the 1920s due to their near extinction, but there are Caribou Inuit archaeological sites which contain large quantities of musk-ox bone, suggesting that they were previously an important part of the diet (see Barr 1991; Friesen & Stewart 2004: 36-38).

Fish were the other major supply which augmented the stores of caribou during the winter, and there was a heavy reliance upon Arctic char (Donald Uluadluak and Mark Kalluak in Dawson et al. 2006: 61-63). Char were generally procured at fishing weirs called *saputit*, which were designed to trap large numbers of the fish as they spawned. The char, once trapped, would be killed using three-pronged fishing leisters called *kakivak* (Mark Kalluak in Dawson et al. 2006: 62; Birket-Smith 1929a: 118-119). *Saputit* were used during the spring run of char to the ocean from the lakes, but the primary fishing season was the fall spawn when the larger char travelled upstream to the lakes for the winter (Bennett & Rowley 2004: 252; Birket-Smith 1929a: 118-119) This usually took place during August to September, coinciding with the autumn caribou hunt (Burch 1986: 121). Trout and other lake fish were generally caught in nets or with bone hooks attached to sinew lines (Birket-Smith 1929a: 117-118, 123). In addition, ice fishing was occasionally practiced once stores of food started to dwindle towards the end of winter (Graham in Williams & Glover 1969:229; Rasmussen 1930:34).

During the spring and summer, the Caribou Inuit also hunted several species of birds and collected their eggs (Donald Uluadluak in Dawson et al. 2006: 31-32). The ptarmigan were particularly important as they arrive before the caribou, early in the spring, just as the last of the winter stores become scarce (Donald Uluadluak and Mark Kalluak in Dawson et al 2006: 16-17, 47; Birket-Smith 1929a: 114; Burch 1986: 122). Birds were hunted using a variety of techniques that range from thrown rocks to snares, bolas, and special arrows (Arima 1984:449; Birket-Smith 1929a: 115-116). Caribou Inuit occasionally used the same technologies to hunt small rodents, and fur bearing carnivores, but none of these were important resources (Birket-Smith 1929a: 113-114; Arima 1984:449). Various berries, plants and seaweed also supplemented the summer diet (Birket-Smith 1929a:135).

The extent to which Caribou Inuit traditionally hunted sea-mammals is a contentious issue. Birket-Smith and Rasmussen reported that whales were never hunted, and that seals and walrus were rarely sought by the Caribou Inuit for a variety of ideological and functional reasons (Birket-Smith 1929a: 125-126; Rasmussen 1930). During their ethnography, however, at least some Caribou Inuit of the Hauniqturmiut, Padlirmiut, and Qaernirmiut, did visit the coast of Hudson Bay to hunt sea-mammals for brief periods during the early spring and summer. In these instances, Caribou Inuit were using techniques similar to those used by Inuit elsewhere in the Arctic. This included the strategy where Bearded and Ringed seals are harpooned through the ice as they surface at breathing holes. Although no longer practiced at the time, Birket-Smith also records that several individuals recalled hunting seals and walrus from kayaks, using the archetypal Inuit culture toggling harpoons and bladder darts (Birket-Smith 1929a: 130-132). Nonetheless, both Birket-Smith and Rasmussen downplayed the hunting of sea-mammals (Birket Smith 1929a; Rasmussen 1930). On this point, Birket-Smith and Rasmussen's observations do not match archaeological and historical evidence. Throughout the historic period, Caribou Inuit are known to have extensively hunted seals, walrus, and whales during the summer (see Chapter 4). As well, archaeological sites at coastal locations, such as the Arviat region, are replete with sea mammal bone indicating that it was a normal facet of subsistence for at least some Caribou Inuit (see Chapter 5) (Bertulli 1990: 7; Dawson 2004: 32; Dawson et al. 2007; Oetelaar 1991: 2).

Caribou Inuit Traders of the Kivalliq

The Caribou Inuit Seasonal Pattern

Overall, the Caribou Inuit pattern of annual movement was governed by the caribou. In the fall, Caribou Inuit would aggregate at inland locations, close to river crossings in order to hunt as many Caribou as possible and prepare the meat for winter storage (Burch 1986: 121). This often coincided with *saputit* fishing for spawning char to supplement winter stores (Birket-Smith 1929a: 113). The Caribou Inuit would then spend the winter at inland locations, usually on lakes in close proximity to their caches (Burch 1986:124-125). Cached food was the primary way in which Caribou Inuit survived the winter, but hunting to supplement the stores was done whenever possible. In the early spring, once the stores were depleted, they would switch to hunting ptarmigan and early arrivals of the Qamanirjuaq herd, as well as fishing the spring run of char (Arima 1984:449; Birket-Smith 1929a: 114; Burch 1986: 122). In some cases, Caribou Inuit would move to the coast in the early spring to hunt sea-mammals (Birket-Smith 1929a: 130-132). In all cases, they would move back inland in anticipation of the fall caribou hunt (Donald Uluadluak & Mark Kalluak in Lyons 2007: 36). So when the Caribou Inuit were not hunting caribou, or living off the stores of caribou, they were 'hanging on' until the ideal conditions to hunt caribou once again arose. As a result, the importance of the fall caribou hunt in understanding the Caribou Inuit culture cannot be stressed enough; it was the time period and strategy that all Caribou Inuit had in common, regardless of what was done in the mean time.

3.4 Social Organization – The Family

The most important unit of Caribou Inuit social organization is the extended family (Burch 1986:116; Damas 1968:146; Lyons 2007:24-27; Williamson 1974: 31-32). This is probably the source of difficulty for anthropologists attempting to understand the hierarchy of sub-groups within Caribou Inuit culture, because rather than identify with such sub-groups, social commitment was directed almost entirely upon the extended family (Williamson 1974: 31). The 'extended family' does not necessarily include any individual that can be linked through kinship, but rather the nuclear relatives that one relied upon on a day-to-day basis[6] (Arima 1984: 454-456). Caribou Inuit remained in close proximity to their extended family throughout their lives (Burch 1986: 116).

All of the hunting techniques, technologies, and subsistence strategies used by the Caribou Inuit were useless without group cooperation. Survival was not a simple matter of hunters returning with food for the family; skins had to be prepared for clothing, tents, and kayaks; caribou had to be scared through drive lanes towards the hunters; carcasses of lanced caribou had to be retrieved, processed, and dried; fish had to be caught, gutted and cured; fuel had to be stored for the winter; etc (Birket-Smith 1929a). For the Caribou Inuit, the extended family was the unit through which all of these, and other, critical tasks were organized. Everything was shared equally within the family. This interdependence gave individuals a strong sense of loyalty towards their family; the very meaning of life, to the Caribou Inuit, was to perpetuate the family (Williamson 1974: 31-32, 42-43).

The Extended Family – Kinship

The importance of perpetuation and solidarity of the extended family is apparent in the kinship patterns of the Caribou Inuit. Marriages were usually arranged for children at a very early age by their parents and grandparents, though this did not necessarily imply a life-long arrangement (Arima 1984: 454-455; Burch 1986: 116-117; Steenhoven 1955a: 40-41). The ideal format was an exchange of cousins, thus building another layer of kinship upon that which already existed. Burch points out that if followed to its logical conclusion, this strategy would result in a situation where large closely-related families would develop (Burch 1986:116). In practice however, family sizes were highly variable, from three individuals to three dozen, and exogamous marriages, often between the various Caribou Inuit sub-groupings, accounted for as much as a quarter of all marriages (Arima 1984: 454; Rasmussen 1930; 11-23). Polygyny was fairly common, and Birket-Smith reported that around one fifth of all married men had two wives or more, though three was considered excessive (Birket-Smith 1929a: 67-68). Ancestry was traced bilineally, and the residence of married couples could be arranged around either side of the family with a tendency towards patrilocality (Arima 1984: 455; Vallee 1967:61).

3.5 Leadership and Decision Making – The Political Process

The concept of leadership in Caribou Inuit society is of particular interest in this study. Related to the lack of inter-family hierarchy or band-level political structure is the fact that leadership occurred primarily within the extended family. This left inter-family politics in a fairly chaotic state, and families that could not get along either had to fight or separate. Within families however, there was a very structured hierarchy that generally conformed to concepts of age and seniority (Burch 1986:120; Williamson 1974: 29, 41). The elderly were individuals who had survived, and, by doing so, had demonstrated intelligence and gained a great deal of experience which were highly valued and respected at the level of the family (Birket-Smith 1929a: 258-259). Williamson goes so far as to suggest that authority and seniority were synonymous (Williamson 1974: 32). Knowledge and intelligence, both equated with age, were the two critical qualities in the Caribou Inuit concept of leadership (Donald Suluk in Bennett & Rowley 2004: 98). Indeed, the Inuktitut word for leader, '*ihumatak*', literally translates as 'one who takes thought' (Arima 1984: 455; Burch 1986:119; Steenhoven 1955a:35, 48; Vallee 1967: Williamson 1974: 21).

---

[6] Eugene Arima provides a Caribou Inuit kinship terminology map (Arima 1984: 456)

The *Ihumatak* has tended to be portrayed by anthropologists as the patriarch of the family, normally of middle to older age, endowed with wisdom, but also physical prowess and considerable hunting skill and ability to provide for the family (see Arima 1984: 455; Burch 1986: 119; Steenhoven 1955b: 14; Vallee 1967: 82). Indeed, such individuals figure prominently in the ethno-historical literature (see Chapter 4). The translation of '*ihumatak*', however, contains no connotation of physical strength. Williamson suggests that while such individuals may have at times performed the role of a leader, it is more often the case that such an individual would be better described as an accepted spokesperson for the will of a family rather than an authority. The presentation of such a spokesman, or 'camp boss', was particularly functional for public interaction with European traders, missionaries, and perhaps anthropologists and other government agents, who expected to deal with such an individual (Williamson 1974: 41-42).

Family solidarity in the decision making process was critical. Families were constantly in a state of committee and discussion regarding such topics as 'when to move camp?' or 'where to go next?'. The freedom of speech about such topics was due to the intimacy of the family with each other, and a collective intimacy with the environmental situation (Birket-Smith 1929a: 95; Vallee 1967: 80-82; Williamson 1974:48). For example, every member of the family understands the implication when the hunters return after a failed excursion, and every person knows the field of options and the likely solution. Leadership then, is often merely the talent of an individual to articulate the consensual knowledge – usually in deference to the opinions of the elderly (Birket-Smith 1929a: 259; Donald Suluk in Bennett & Rowley 2004:98). This talent was not exclusive to men. Many women, especially those that had passed through menopause, were particularly strong in personality and could be very vocal in the decision making process (Steenhoven 1955a: 35; Vallee 1967: 80-82; Williamson 1974: 47-49).

3.6 Leadership and Decision Making – The Ideological Basis

Caribou Inuit also perceived the world in ways that are very different when compared to the rest of the Arctic. All things were delineated by their association with the land or the ocean. Items that belonged to the ocean, such as sea mammal products, had to be treated with the utmost caution; there were many rules and taboos that governed such materials when they were near caribou crossings or fishing weirs (Arima 1984: 455-457; Keith 2004: 51-52; Rasmussen 1930: 48-65, 79). Such constraints could only be negotiated by the bearers of amulets, and leadership in such issues ultimately fell to the *Angakut*[7] (Williamson 1974:26).

---

[7] '*Angakok*' is the circum-polar Inuktitut word for 'shaman'. '*Angakut*' refers to more than two.

Caribou Inuit *Angakut* were unique in their powers; they were primarily healers, and unlike other Inuit *Angakut*, they could not control the movements or behaviours of animals; at most, an *Angakok* could separate their soul from body, and travel ahead, down the routes of travel to see if animals were there (Donald Uluadluak & Mark Kalluak in Lyons 2007: 34; Rasmussen 1930: 46-47; Williamson 1974:27). This was strongly related to the belief that *Pinga*, the female guardian of all life, existed primarily to receive and reincarnate the souls of both humans and animals once they died (Arima 1984: 457; Rasmussen 1930: 50). *Pinga* did not interfere with or control the caribou, who were masters of their own selves (Rasmussen 1930: 49). Coercion of the supernatural was therefore useless, and made the role of the *Angakut* in Caribou Inuit society quite different than in other coastal Inuit groups (Rasmussen 1930: 54-55).

In roles of leadership, Caribou Inuit *Angakut* certainly had authority and were often the most influential persons in an extended family, but the principle was more akin to the concept of the *ihumatak*. *Angakut* could be either male or female (Rasmussen 1930: 56). While their insights were seldom questioned, their decisions rarely ran counter to the consensus of the family in the first place (Williamson 1974: 41-45). Even the most famous of *Angakut* were exceptionally humble about their powers. During his travels, Rasmussen heard many stories about a powerful *Angakok* named Igjugârjuk. Eventually Rasmussen arrived at Igjugârjuk's camp and questioned him about his fame. Igjugârjuk's reply was simply that he was an "ordinary and ignorant man who knew nothing" (Rasmussen 1930: 39). The Caribou Inuit *Angakut* were less inclined towards the public displays of magic and power that were common at social aggregations elsewhere in the Arctic. Although such performances did occasionally occur, they were generally received with scepticism (Lyons 2007: 23; Rasmussen 1930: 54, 58-59; Steenhoven 1955c: 19-21). Most shamanic practices tended to be more private and involved segregation from society. During a noviciate's training, they frequently spent large quantities of time in secluded snow houses, having carefully arranged the snow so that there were no footprints in the vicinity (Donald Uluadluak in Lyons 2007: 34; Rasmussen 1930: 51-53). Indeed, Igjugârjuk's strategy to heal a sick individual did not require any theatrics; he would simply leave the camp for a period to meditate (Rasmussen 1930:55).

3.7 Caribou Inuit Origins and Development

Because of their uniqueness, the origins and development of the Caribou Inuit culture has been a central debate in Arctic archaeology. The general consensus is that the characteristic preference for interior life is a fairly recent adaptation that may have developed entirely within the historic period. There are however, two competing theories regarding the ancestral origins. One theory, originally proposed by Elmer Harp, is that the Caribou Inuit developed *in situ* from Thule populations that moved south along the coast of Hudson Bay, and then into the interior (Harp 1961: 73-74; 1963). At the very least, Thule populations were present in the northern Kivalliq. For example, several Thule sites have been reported on the Meliadine River, which is to the west of Rankin Inlet (see Figure 1) (Clark 1977; Linnamae & Clark 1976). A crucial element of this model is that the development of Caribou Inuit culture may have matured during the historic period, but was part of a cultural process that had its roots in the prehistory of the area.

The second theory was first suggested by William E. Taylor and then popularized by Ernst Burch (Burch 1978: 2; Taylor 1965:14-15; 1972: 42). Taylor and Burch point out that although Thule populations were present in the Kivalliq, there is no evidence of a transitional stage, which might be expected given the radical differences in Caribou Inuit culture. In their model, a 'founder society' migrated to the Kivalliq in the late 17th century, likely originating in the Copper Inuit area (see Figure 1). The 'founder society' were a coastal people, who through the process of interacting with the fur trade, acquiring such technologies as the gun, were able to move inland during the early to mid 19th century which led to the formation of the classical Caribou Inuit culture studied by ethnographers in the early 1900s. Other researchers, however, point out that the Caribou Inuit exhibited a general ambivalence towards European trade, and were technologically capable of interior subsistence without European technologies (Damas 1988:105). The support for Burch and Taylor's theory comes primarily from information gained in the Hudson Bay Company Archives (HBCA), and has never been proven archaeologically, although Yvon Csonka points out that it has never been disproved either (Csonka 1994: 24-25).

If the uniqueness of Caribou Inuit culture owes its existence to the Fur Trade, then the defining linguistic, technological, social, and ideological intricacies were no older than 100 years when first documented in the early 1900s. Yet anthropological research, both current and old, consistently reports a well-formed and deeply-rooted cultural tradition which has pervaded even into the present (Birket-Smith 1929a; Henderson 1997; Keith 2004; Rasmussen 1930). There is a persistent social memory of a more traditional era, where interior life was conducted without European goods (see Keith 2004; Rasmussen 1930: 40-41). This has informed a number of recent projects which combine oral history with archaeology. This includes Max Friesen, Darren Keith, and Andrew Stewart who have worked primarily with the Harvaqtarmiut, Yvon Csonka with the Ahiarmiut, and most recently Peter Dawson and Natasha Lyons with the Padlirmiut (Dawson 2005; Dawson et al. 2006; Dawson et al 2007; Friesen & Stewart 1994; Friesen et al. 2000; Friesen & Stewart 2004; Keith 1998; Lyons 2007). Given the amount of new knowledge that each of these projects is producing, anthropological interpretations regarding the Caribou Inuit are probably on the cusp of being reordered, and are likely to focus more on internal cultural dynamics.

Chapter 4 – Caribou Inuit and the Fur Trade

4.1 Introduction

This chapter examines the origin, development, and nature of the relationship between the Caribou Inuit and European trade. In general, the format is a sequential presentation of significant events that are apparent in historical sources. The ultimate objective, however, is to consider the various ways that new economic possibilities affected Inuit individuals, how those individuals reacted to new situations, and the cultural consequences of the choices that they made. To accomplish this, the discussion occasionally departs from a chronological structure in order to include Inuit perspectives such as stories of European origins and the profiles of Caribou Inuit traders.

Chapter 4 necessarily draws upon a variety of epistemological sources. The primary source for historical information is the Hudson Bay Company Archives (HBCA)[8], which contain information regarding Inuit interaction in trade-post journals, account books, ship logs, annual reports, correspondence, maps, and explorers' diaries. The history is occasionally supplemented by ethnographic and archaeological sources that concern the Caribou Inuit. The combination of history, ethnography, and archaeology permits a detailed examination of significant events, patterns of interaction, and most importantly - real historical people. These sources intersect with their living descendants, Padlirmiut Elders from Arviat, whose memories are also used to examine the profiles of several individuals who acted as intermediaries between Caribou Inuit culture and the HBC.

4.2 1611-1717 Early Explorations of Hudson Bay

During the 1600s, the West coast of Hudson Bay was visited six times by various explorers (see Table 5). None of these explorers reported contact with the Inuit, but it is possible that they were themselves sighted by the Inuit. The lack of Inuit sightings by explorers in the 17th century has occasionally been used as a line of evidence to suggest that the coast was uninhabited during that period (see Burch 1978:4-8; Burch 1979:198-201; Stewart 1994:44-45). However, it is equally possible that the explorers and Inuit missed each other on every single occasion. The explorations only occurred during the peak summer months, and covered vast distances of previously unmapped coast line (see Burch 1979:199; Cooke & Holland 1978:26-53). The coast from Churchill to Repulse Bay alone is over 1000 km, and Caribou Inuit only congregate at a small number of locations during the summer months. Most of the explorers were primarily concerned with mapping the coast line, yet major features, such as Chesterfield Inlet, were not discovered during the 17th century indicating that the coast was not thoroughly explored by any of the expeditions. It is an entirely reasonable possibility that Inuit were overlooked as well.

Table 5 Early Hudson Bay Explorers (Cooke & Holland 1978: 26-53)

Explorer	Dates Present in Hudson Bay
Henry Hudson	1610-1611
Thomas Button	1612-1613
Jens Munk	1619-1620
Luke Foxe	1631
Thomas James	1631
Henry Kelsey	1689

4.3 1717-1790 Early Period of HBC Trade

Churchill Post[9] was established in 1717 by James Knight, servant of the HBC (see Figure 6). The Company wanted to trace the sources of Native copper and explore the possibility of a Northwest Passage (Hearne 1958: *lx*). Both of these required further exploration of Hudson Bay and therefore contact with the Inuit. During the period of 1717-1790, primary goals for post-masters included fostering a secure trade relationship between the Inuit and the Company, as well as collecting as much information about the area as possible (Fossett 2001:124; Williams & Glover 1969: *xlii*). As a result, the defining characteristic of interaction between the HBC and the Caribou Inuit during the early period is that the trade was brought to the Inuit; trade sloops were sent along the coast to summer villages where large numbers of Inuit aggregated to hunt seals and whales. The sloops were often run at a loss to the Company, and the trade itself was anything but lucrative; it was mostly conducted in order to draw the Inuit into a closer relationship (Robson 1759:64-66). Another important characteristic of the early period is that there was a great deal of conflict and tension between the Chipewyan and the Inuit. The source of that conflict may be rooted in prehistory, but the events that occurred in the 1700s are inextricably linked to the presence of the HBC (Smith & Burch 1979:76).

---

[8] The HBCA materials are housed at the Provincial Archives of Manitoba (PAM). In this report, all HBCA sources are referenced according to the official PAM HBCA formatting policy. In text citations include only the HBCA reference number. For example purposes, (B.42/a/141) provides the reader with the adequate information to access the document in question. All such references to be assumed to be preceded by the prefix 'PAM HBCA' even though it does not appear in the text.

[9] Churchill was renamed Fort Prince of Wales in 1719 by Richard Ward (Cooke & Holland 1978:53). The two names are synonymous in this report.

Caribou Inuit Traders of the Kivalliq

Figure 6 Hudson Bay 1717-1900 A.D.

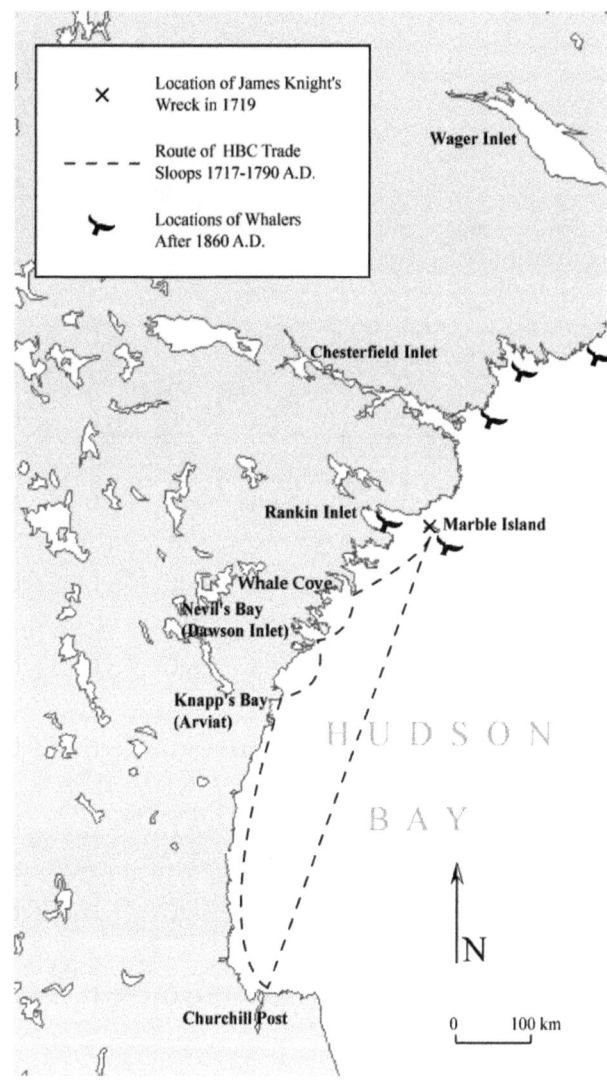

Chronology

Knight founded Churchill on the location at which he believed Jens Munk[10] had wintered at a hundred years earlier (Knight 1932:113). A wooden fort was built there and two of the ships that had accompanied him, the *Success* and the *Prosperous*, stayed at Churchill to be used as trade and expedition sloops (Cooke & Holland 1978:52). Knight brought with him several servants of the Company as well as some Chipewyan guides and hunters whom the Company referred to as "Home Indians". On the basis of information provided by Chipewyan informants, Knight had been under the impression that Churchill was a location that was frequently visited by the Inuit. The advance party that he sent, comprised solely of Chipewyan, claimed to have been ambushed by the Inuit whilst crossing the mouth of the Churchill River. Six of the nine Chipewyan were killed by the Inuit who apparently had a village in the area (Kenney 1932:59; Knight 1932:114). Indeed it can be seen in his 1717 journal, that Knight constantly expected the arrival of the Inuit even though they never came. In that journal, Knight suggests that the first fort was built on top of an Inuit village, including what appeared to be a boat-building workshop and several graves (Knight 1932:116). Although this has never been proven archaeologically, it seems to have been a belief on the part of HBC staff throughout the historic period that Churchill had been occupied by the Inuit before the presence of HBC Home Indians drove them to the North. For example, when rebuilding the foundations of the fort in the mid-1700s, Joseph Robson[11] states that artifacts that are diagnostic of Inuit culture, such as stone kettles and pots were uncovered during construction (Robson 1759:64).

First contact with the Inuit did not occur until 1718 when the Company sent David Vaughan[12] up the coast to meet potential patrons. The encounter was brief, and the Inuit displayed little awe or enthusiasm for trade (B.239/b/1). Between 1718 and 1722, the Company sent six ships up the coast, all of which made further contact with the Inuit. This included James Knight's ill fated voyage which disappeared in 1719 (see Figure 6) (Beattie & Geiger 1993:75-76; Kenney 1932:82). Knight had been on an expedition to find the source of Native copper as well as investigate the Northwest Passage. It was not until 1769, that Samuel Hearne received an eye-witness account, from the Inuit, that Knight had been wrecked on Marble Island (Beattie & Geiger 1993: 93-94). The Inuit there had attempted to assist Knight and his crew of thirty men, but they had all died off by 1721 (Hearne 1958: *lxii*).

Renée Fossett notes that the first contact and trade with the Inuit on the coast of Hudson's Bay was very different than the way it occurred in other parts of the Arctic (Fossett 2001:93). Elsewhere, trade was met with joyous festivities and groups of Inuit gathered around the ships for days after the trade was complete, dancing and playing games with the crews. Conversely, the opposite was sometimes true, as in the case of Frobisher, where explorers and traders were often met with violence and hostility. On the West coast of Hudson's Bay, the Inuit seemed indifferent to the trade, as well as the presence of the traders. The exchange was fairly simple - metal knives and cutting tools for whale oil and walrus ivory. After transaction, the Inuit showed little interest in the Company traders and left immediately (B.239/b/1). Discouraged by the paucity of Inuit trade, the HBC sloops were stopped in 1722, and there was no direct contact with the Inuit until the voyages were resumed in 1737 (B.239/b/2; Cooke & Holland 1978:55-60; Fossett 2001:94).

---

[10] Jens Munk was a Danish explorer sent to search for a Northwest Passage in 1619. His expedition spent the winter at the mouth of the Churchill River. During that winter, all but 3 of his 65 men succumbed to scurvy (Cooke & Holland 1978:28).

[11] Joseph Robson was a company employee who specialized in building forts. He was at Churchill between 1733-36 (Kenney 1932:95; Robson 1759)

[12] David Vaughn was an HBC trade sloop captain from 1718-1722 (Cooke & Holland 1978:55-56).

One incident that is particularly illuminating on the whereabouts and activities of the Chipewyan during this period occurred in 1725. Over a hundred Chipewyan arrived at Churchill from the North. They said that they had been attacked by the Inuit on or near Marble Island (see Figure 6). Several Chipewyan had been killed, and they seemed irritated with the post-master for suggesting that they befriend the Inuit (B.42/a/5). This incident occurred far outside of the territory that would normally be associated with the Chipewyan during this period. It can be noted that Marble Island is not too far from where the northernmost boundary of the Caribou Inuit themselves would normally be placed. Smith and Burch (1979:80) point out that the Chipewyan may have regularly travelled even further North during this period; the guides that were with John Scroggs[13] in 1722 were familiar with the Roes Welcome Sound area, and claimed that they could reach their own country with a two or three day walk (see Figure 1). It is difficult to speculate the reasons why the Chipewyan would travel so far beyond the tree line. It is likely however, that their familiarity with the area came from their use of the river ways of the region.

In 1737, the Company resumed its interest in finding a Northwest Passage, and sent another trade ship up the coast (Cooke & Holland 1978:60). This time, the trade was a lot better and the Inuit were promised that the ship would return to Whale Cove the following year. In 1738 however, when it did return, there were no Inuit to be found (Davies & Johnson 1965: 253-58). Between 1739 and 1744, the company sent another four ships to trade, which were met with mixed success (Cooke & Holland 1978: 60-62). In some years the trade was very poor, but in others the company managed to procure as much as several tons of whale oil (Robson 1759:66). Although the Inuit seemed more enthusiastic than before, the trade was mostly run at a loss to the Company. For example, in 1744 the HBC traders approached a single-tent camp North of Knapp's Bay[14], and traded 14 finger rings, 13 knives, 4 awls, 2 ice chisels, a double edged scraper, and 1 lb. of glass beads, all in exchange for a single bag of seal oil (see Figure 6) (B.42/a/46). The HBC observed that the Inuit were hunting whales, walrus, and seals, using seal skin kayaks. The Inuit primarily traded oil, blubber, baleen, and ivory – all coastal products – but it was noted that the whaling season was only nine weeks long (Robson 1759:66).

One point that suggests the Inuit economy was much broader than what they were trading is that the coast seemed to have been entirely abandoned on some years, and Inuit were presumably inland. It was noted repeatedly by Company employees during this period that the Inuit would prove to be invaluable trade partners if only the sloops were sent more regularly (Davies &

Chapter 4 – Caribou Inuit and the Fur Trade

Johnson 1965: 247-260; Fossett 2001:94; Robson 1759). In 1744 however, the trade sloops were again stopped (Cook & Holland 1978:64).

In 1750, the trade sloops were resumed and were sent up the coast annually until 1790 (see Figure 6) (Cooke & Holland 1978: 68-110). This time, the trade started with the usual ambivalence, but led into a series of strange incidents between 1753 and 1755. In 1753, Captain Walker[15] was not met with disinterest, but rather violence (Fossett 2001:102-103). The following is a summary of the incidents that he recorded in the 1753 logbook of the *Churchill*, a trade sloop, of which he was Captain (B.42/a/41). At Knapp's Bay, none of the Inuit seemed particularly interested in trading, and when they did, they did so under very strange conditions. One group insisted that they be lent a boat and some sailors to go to their caches. The sailors were gone for nearly a whole day, and when they returned, they had only a small quantity of seal oil. Over the next couple of days, large numbers of Inuit kept arriving from inland and from the north, all of which refused to trade. Several more strange requests were made which would have again separated the crew, so the sloop moved to Dawson Inlet. The sloop did not stay long there either. Again there were large numbers of Inuit who acted very aggressively and threatened to stab one of the sailors.

At Whale Cove, there were over 100 Inuit when the sloop arrived. There were repeated attempts to board the sloop which had to be guarded by armed sailors at all times. In one incident, a man actually got aboard and stabbed Captain Walker in the leg. Two days later, after another attempt to board the ship, the Inuit made a raft and brought some women out, abandoning them in the lifeboats. Walker threatened to cut the boats loose, and the women were removed. The next day, there was yet another boarding attempt which was repelled only by the order to sink their kayaks if necessary. That party returned to the shore where they made threatening gestures by sharpening their lances and pointing them at the ship. There was a second boarding attempt the same day which was again repelled, and Walker started to prepare the ship to leave. As they were preparing, over 300 Inuit were on the beach making threatening gestures at the ship, but the sailors managed to leave without further incident (see Fossett 2001:102-103).

The exact causes and motives behind the aggressive behaviour on the part of the Inuit are not apparent, but there are several implications that are important. First, the aggression appears to have been organized. All of the Inuit in the communities at Knapp's Bay, Dawson Inlet, and Whale Cove, were passive one year and then aggressive the next; there are no extenuating conditions that could account for a coincidental reaction. Although the provocation is not perceptible, there must have been communication and agreement among those communities to greet the trade

---

[13] John Scroggs was an HBC trade sloop captain during the 1720s (Cooke & Holland 1978:55-56).
[14] Knapp's Bay was the name used by the HBC to describe the area that is now referred to as Arviat (G.4/26). The two names are synonymous in this report.

[15] Captain Walker commanded the *Churchill*, an HBC trade sloop, between 1750-54 (B.42/1/41-46).

sloop in the aggressive manner that they did. Another inference is that the number of Inuit living in the region was much larger than what was normally visible to the traders from the shore. This may indicate that there were also large numbers of Inuit that normally lived inland, and had no direct contact with the HBC during the 1700s.

The nature of the aggression seems to indicate that the Inuit were less interested in procuring European goods, and more interested in challenging and attacking them. If it was the goods they wanted, it seems reasonable that the Inuit would have been more amenable to trade, or at least it might be expected that they would have used the repeated boarding attempts to steal items from the *Churchill*. Infrequent as it was, the Inuit had over 30 years of trade experience to know the protocol for procuring European goods; their actions and behaviours in 1753 seem to have been directed at the very presence of the *Churchill* and her crew rather than their profession as traders. The unknown circumstances which led to the events of 1753 were probably social or ideological. At Whale Cove in particular, it would seem there was also some element of symbolism in the aggressive behaviour. It is unclear why women were placed in the *Churchill's* lifeboats considering that the Inuit had attempted to repel the traders not an hour earlier. This action combined with the gestures and chanting baffled the HBC traders, but probably contained a unified message that the Inuit were trying to communicate.

Whatever the provocation in 1753, Captain Walker's return in 1754 was met with a completely opposite reaction. Inuit were much fewer in number, with 150 for the entire coast, and they were very eager to trade (B.42/a/43). Particularly interesting is the fact that in addition to sea mammals, the Inuit also traded large quantities of caribou meat. There was a complete reversal in attitude towards trade as well, and the Inuit eagerly bought what was offered, literally taking the pots and pans from the galley by the time they were finished (B.42/a/43 & 45). Regional communication and organization is again implied by the uniform transition, and the rest of the Inuit must have returned inland.

One of the most notorious events in the history of Hudson Bay is the massacre at Knapp's Bay of 1755. In this incident, Captain John Bean[16] was travelling northwards toward Knapp's Bay (B.42/a/47). South of Knapp's Bay, the sloop was smoke signalled from the shore by a group of Chipewyan who wished to trade. The Company expected at that point in time for the Chipewyan to travel to Churchill from the interior, and the sloops had been ordered to give strict preference to Inuit trade. So the sloop ignored the Chipewyan and carried on to Knapp's Bay where they traded with a group of 18 Inuit. As the ship was leaving they heard a volley of gunfire, but continued on their trade route not knowing what had happened - it was not until November that several Chipewyan told the post-master at Churchill what transpired. Having been greatly offended at being ignored by the sloop, the signalling Chipewyan had stalked the ship along the coast until it arrived at Knapp's Bay. They had then hid behind some rocks and watched the trade between the Company and the Inuit. Once the sloop had left they attacked the Inuit camp and killed all of them. The detailed account in the post-journals is quite vivid and has been described elsewhere (B.42/a/47; Fossett 2001:106). In 1769, Hearne suggested that a partial reason for the severity of the attack had to do with the death of one of the Chipewyan leaders which had been attributed to sorcery and magic on the part of the Inuit (Hearne 1958: 217; Smith & Burch 1979:81).

It might be expected that the response to this incident on the part of the Inuit would be one of retaliation given their earlier hostilities. However, by 1762, a truce was declared between the Inuit and Chipewyan at Knapp's Bay (B.42/a/58; Williams & Glover 1969: *xlv*). The truce seems to have worked for that location. By 1765, the Chipewyan were present at Knapp's Bay in larger numbers than the Inuit until 1782. Fossett notes that the ratio was typically three or four Chipewyan to every Inuk (Fossett 2001:107). An important note is that this group of Chipewyan was clearly a different group than those who had committed the massacre in 1755. The Inuit were also possibly a different group than those that had been present at the massacre as well. For several years after 1754, no Inuit were seen at Knapp's Bay and it cannot be certain that those who eventually moved back were the same as those that had left (Hearne 1958:217). The truce itself was brokered by a Chipewyan named "Captain Hissty" who was described as a "Home Indian", whereas it was the "Away Indians" who had done the killing (Fossett 2001:107).

In other parts of the Kivalliq however, hostilities continued; there are several incidents where war parties, both Chipewyan and Cree, were deterred at Churchill from proceeding north (B.42/a/78; B239/a/5). The final incident involving bloodshed was the massacre at Bloody Falls, on the Coppermine River, witnessed by Samuel Hearne in 1771 (see Figure 7) (Hearne 1958: 94-111). The cessation of hostilities after Bloody Falls is often attributed to the small pox epidemics which drew the Chipewyan to the south in the years preceding 1780 (see Fossett 2001: 111-113). Another possible factor was that the Inuit population had recently become armed.

From the time that regular trade sloops were run in 1750, it was normal for several Inuit boys from Knapp's Bay, Whale Cove, and Marble Island, to spend the winter at Churchill as servants of the Company. Such boys were taught English, Chipewyan, and Cree, and were used by the company as ambassadors of trade. Hearne notes that they were instrumental in allowing members of each ethnic group to meet with each other (Hearne 1958:218). The Inuit finally began to procure fire arms during the 1760s which was largely due to the efforts of Andrew Graham who was the post-master at the

---

[16] Captain Bean replaced Captain Walker as the commander of the *Churchill* in 1755 (B.42/a/47).

time. During the winter he trained the Inuit boys at Churchill how to load, fire, and maintain the flint-lock muskets that could be traded for through the company (Graham 1969: 236). It was at this point the Inuit began to trade for fire arms, and by the early 1800s, almost every Inuit man owned a gun (Damas 1988:105). A possible consequence of acquiring fire arms is that the Inuit were drawn into a closer relationship with the HBC; muskets need powder, shot, flints, and occasional maintenance.

During this time, the trade between the HBC and the Inuit became much more lucrative for both parties and the relationship became stronger. The sloops visited Knapp's Bay, Whale Cove, Chesterfield Inlet, and Marble Island every year after 1750 (see Figure 6). Population estimates conducted by the HBC sloop captains were highly variable, normally between 150 to 200 individuals between Knapp's Bay and Rankin Inlet (Fossett 2001:112). Occasionally, the population was dramatically higher; as noted already in 1753 for example, the trade sloop was met by very large numbers of Inuit at each stop, with over 300 at Whale Cove alone. After several years of regular trade, Andrew Graham[17] estimated that there were about 500 Inuit that lived in communities along the coast during the summer (Graham 1969:213, 238). The fact that those numbers could jump so dramatically in a single year is probably a strong indication that there were also large numbers of Inuit that normally lived in the interior as well.

In 1790, the last trade sloop was sent north (Cooke & Holland 1978: 110). The HBC had faced a number of challenges in the preceding decade including a brief takeover of Churchill by the French from 1782 to 1784, who destroyed most of the fort (Glover 1958: *xxxix*). The Churchill trade throughout the 1780s was very poor. The Chipewyan had suffered a massive epidemic and had little to part with (Fossett 2001:111). Inuit trade was also reduced; in 1780, for example, only 35 families were encountered along the whole coast, none of which had anything to trade. Weather, along with the loss of community members to an accident were cited by the Company as probable causes (B.42/a/101). Trade sloops also found it difficult to locate the Inuit during these years. In 1788 Inuit were not in their regular summer villages; Knapp's Bay and Marble Island were abandoned, their occupants having moved temporarily to Whale Cove and Nevil's Bay (B.42/a/113). The HBC could no longer afford to take the trade to the Inuit, and the sloops were ceased. If the Caribou Inuit wanted to continue trade, they would have to travel all the way to Churchill to do so.

Chapter 4 – Caribou Inuit and the Fur Trade

4.4 European Impact on Caribou Inuit Culture in the Early Period of HBC Trade

The actual impact that Europeans incurred upon Caribou Inuit culture during the 1700s is a contentious issue in anthropology. This is mostly because the 1700s is a pivotal time period in theories regarding the origins and development of Caribou Inuit culture. For example, in Burch's theory, it is not until the early/mid 1800s that groups of coastal Inuit moved inland and began spending the entire year in the interior of the Kivalliq (Burch 1978:13-14; Burch 1986:113-114; Smith & Burch 1979:83-85). In this and similar models, the defining feature of Caribou Inuit culture, a preference for interior life, did not develop until they had been in contact with European traders for over a hundred years.

In some cases, European technologies, such as guns and fish hooks, are credited with allowing Caribou Inuit to adapt to interior life in the first place (Clark 1975: 26, 131-132, 151-152; Williams & Glover 1969: *li-lii*). Stewart, however, points out that even in the late-historic period, much of the caribou hunting was done with lances and spears, and that Inuit in general are technologically capable of residing inland even when they do not; fire-arms need not be considered a critical technology (Stewart 1994: 46-48). Vallee also observes that the fire-arms did not actually replace traditional technologies as the bow and arrow were used by Caribou Inuit into the 1920s (Vallee 1967:35). Even Burch downplays the actual role of Europeans in Caribou Inuit development (Burch 1986:114). Damas and Williamson elaborate on this latter view by suggesting that the degree of European influence was small until the 1900s, when trade posts expanded into the Kivalliq, and the fur trade replaced the traditional economy by bringing the Inuit into a debit-credit relationship with European traders (Damas 1988; Williamson 1974:66-69).

The fact that the HBC struggled to interest the Caribou Inuit in trade throughout the 1700s is perhaps the best way to measure the consequence of European presence. If the introduction of European trade had a profound effect on Caribou Inuit culture, then the Inuit reaction should have been more proactive, either by embracing the new economy, or through aggressive resistance. Yet the Inuit that were encountered by the trade sloops were mostly interested in their own affairs with a couple of exceptions that have been discussed. It seems intuitive that the Inuit would have been more interested the new materials and products introduced by the Europeans. So why was it so difficult for the HBC to incorporate the Caribou Inuit? To explore this question, it is useful to examine the events of the 1700s from an Inuit point of view.

4.5 The Development of Caribou Inuit/European Relations

In considering Caribou Inuit perceptions of Europeans during the early historic period, it must be recalled that their first major interaction was with James

---

[17] Andrew Graham was the Churchill post-master in the 1760s. He made extensive ethnological notes regarding the Hudson Bay region which were organized and published by the Hudson Bay Records society in 1969.

Knight and his wrecked crew at Marble Island. The nature of the encounter was recited vividly to Samuel Hearne in 1769 by Inuit Elders who could recall the incident 51 years earlier (Beattie & Geiger 1993:93-94; Hearne 1958: *lxii*). Knight's ships had been damaged by a storm and were driven into a rocky harbour from which they could not be salvaged. The survivors, numbering about fifty, built a shelter and attempted to survive the winter. Upon returning to Marble Island in 1720, the Inuit found that many of the survivors had died of starvation, and those who hadn't, were desperately trying to build a boat. Their number had been reduced to twenty as they attempted to survive the second winter as castaways. The Inuit gave them supplies of seal and whale blubber, apparently trading for European items such as clothing and nails. The dwindling survivors managed to make it through the following summer, but were all dead before the onset of winter in 1721. In 1720, on a voyage to trade with the Inuit and look for Knight, Captain John Hancock[18] learned from the Inuit that Knight was stranded on Marble Island, indicating that news of Knight and his fate had spread among the Inuit, and preceded first contact, with the exception of David Vaughan's brief encounter in 1718 (Cooke & Holland 1978:54; Kenney 1932:82). In 1722, John Scroggs noted that relics of Knight's ship could be found amongst Inuit as far south as Whale Cove; information regarding the wrecked crew presumably accompanied the traded items (Kenney 1932: 83-84). First impressions are important, and it would seem that the Caribou Inuit were first introduced to Europeans as helpless, washed-up sailors who were entirely dependant on the Inuit for food. In this context, it is no small wonder that they appeared to be ambivalent to trade.

In Caribou Inuit culture, there is a popular story concerning the origins of Europeans. The story is particularly useful in considering the ways in which the Inuit behaved towards the Europeans during the 1700s. It has been recorded a number of times, first in 1915 by Christian Leden[19], and the story certainly has a much earlier origin (Donald Uluadluak in Lyons 2007: 35; Kalluak 1974; Leden 1990: 262). The following is the version told to Knud Rasmussen in 1922 by Igjugârjuk[20], the famous shaman.

How the White-men and Indians First Came

'There once was a girl who refused all the men who wished to marry her. At last her father was so annoyed with her that he went off with her to an island with his dog. He paddled away with her to the island of Anarnigtoq (the one that smells of dirt), an island that lies out in lake Háningajoq, not far from Hikoligjuaq (Yathkyed Lake[21]). The dog took the girl to wife, and they lived together on the island, and at last the woman had worn away all the skin from her elbows and knees, so often had she been forced to go down on all fours when the dog wanted to have its way with her. At last she grew pregnant, and brought forth a number of whelps. And the girl's father brought meat to the island that they might not starve. One day, when the young ones were grown up, their mother spoke to them and said: "Next time your grandfather comes over to the island, you are to swim out to him and upset his kayak". The dogs did so, and the grandfather was drowned. Thus the girl took vengeance on her father for having forced her to marry a dog. But now that the grandfather was dead there was no one to bring meat for the dogs, so the girl cut off the soles of her kamiks, and set them out in the water, and working magic over them, set some of the dogs on one sole, saying: "be skilful in all manner of work you undertake".

And the dogs drifted out from the island, and when they had come a little way out in the lake, the sole turned into a ship, and they sailed away to white men's land and turned into white men. And from them, it is said, all the white men came.

But the other dogs the girl placed on the other kamik sole, and letting them drift away from the island, she worked magic and said: "Avenge me on your grandfather, showing yourselves bloodthirsty as often as you meet with human beings."

And the kamik sole was washed ashore, and the dogs wandered off up the country and turned into Itqitlit. From them came all the Indians.'
- (Rasmussen 1930:101)

The content of this story is consistent with the behaviour of the Caribou Inuit during the 1700s; the revelation of the European's existence doesn't seem to have shattered or forever changed the lives of the Inuit. Rather than a highly-advanced culture, whose technologies awed and defied traditional knowledge, it would seem that the Europeans were easily, if not comically, accounted for by the Caribou Inuit. It is interesting to note that this story depicts the Europeans as incidental to the existence of the Inuit themselves. In the Inuit perspective, counter to the historical view, the Europeans came from a known place in Inuit territory and owed their existence to an amusing domestic dispute. Most importantly, the story of European origins is mundane in its magnitude when compared to the epic legends of Inuit origins (see Rasmussen 1930: 97-99).

---

[18] John Hancock was an HBC trade sloop captain in the early 1720s (Cooke & Holland 1978:55).
[19] Christian Leden was a Norwegian ethnographer who travelled extensively amongst the Caribou Inuit between 1913-1916 (Leden 1990).
[20] Igjugârjuk was a Padlirmiut *Angakok* (shaman), and was Knud Rasmussen's primary informant regarding Caribou Inuit intellectual culture. When Rasmussen lived with him in 1922, he was residing inland at Hikoligjuaq Lake the entire year, but had previously lived at Arviat, and had travelled long distances to the Back River, and even Bathurst Inlet (Rasmussen 1930: 8, 54-55).

[21] *Háningajoq* was referred to as *Qablunaarurvik*, an Island in Maguse Lake by Donald Uluadluak and Mark Kalluak during the 2007 Arviat Oral History project (see Figure 1) (see Lyons 2007:35).

Europeans are not depicted as good or bad, but as having a simple mission that they were cast away to complete, returning years later.

This is not to say that the Caribou Inuit did not think the Europeans clever. In another conversation with Rasmussen, Igjugârjuk held European technologies in very high esteem (Rasmussen 1930:40). Specifically referring to the gun, he thought it a remarkable invention that had made Inuit life much easier. Because of the gun, Inuit could procure more than ever as they were able to kill caribou in large numbers under most circumstances of encounter. For comparison, Igjugârjuk described in great detail the techniques that had been used to hunt before the gun was introduced, when bow and arrow were used along with lances and traps. Before any great number of caribou could be killed, they had to be funnelled through cairns and drive lanes or ambushed at river crossings; all of which took a great deal of work and planning. Though very impressed and highly appreciative of the gun, Igjugârjuk concluded by pointing out that he considered the traditional ways of hunting were much more 'gentle' (Rasmussen 1930:40-42). So even after 200 years of Inuit access to European trade, Igjugârjuk had a very firm grasp on what traditional life was like and the ways in which European technologies had supplemented it. Igjugârjuk could have done without his gun if he had to; like his ancestors of the 18th century, he did not perceive a need for dependence upon the Europeans.

When questioned about Chipewyan and Inuit relations during the 1700s, a common explanation for Chipewyan aggression is that they desired Inuit technologies (Louie Angalik in Dawson et al. 2006: 11). This perception may have also extended to the Europeans as well, who were depicted as having a common origin. One thing that must have been apparent to the Inuit about the European traders was that they were entirely reliant on the Inuit in order to conduct their trade; the Europeans were perfectly willing to part with their clever devices in exchange for seals, whales, ivory etc., which they seemed incapable of procuring for themselves. Consider a trade previously mentioned in this chapter, where 14 finger rings, 13 knives, 4 awls, 2 ice chisels, a double edged scraper, and 1 lb of beads were traded to a single person for a small quantity of oil (B.42/a/46). The recipient of that exchange must have wondered what the traders intended to do with the oil to pay that price. It is trade such as this which formed the early relationship between the Company and the Caribou Inuit. From this perspective, it is possible that by trying to coax the Caribou Inuit into a closer relationship at a loss to themselves, the HBC posited the Inuit as technologically, or at least technically superior; products that were normally hunted by the Inuit were worth something to the Europeans, who were incapable of acquiring them for themselves.

In Caribou Inuit culture, an important distinction is made between things that belong to the land, and things that belong to the ocean (Arima 1984: 455-457; Keith 2004: 51-52; Rasmussen 1930: 48-65, 79). An important observation made by Rasmussen is that trade goods, procured from Europeans, were subject to strict rules as they were included in the ocean category (Rasmussen 1930:48). All had to be treated with a great deal of caution, along with other coastal products such as seal skin or walrus meat. This was especially so at caribou crossings, which were places subject to a great deal of protocol (Rasmussen 1930:34). The association of the ocean with trade goods and Europeans in general is deeply routed in the history of interaction. The first Europeans, the dogs from Igjugârjuk's story, were cast away on a kamik that turned into a ship, taking them across the ocean to 'white-men's land'. Upon returning, the first Europeans that contacted the Inuit appeared on ships, or as in the case of Knight's crew, washed ashore on Marble Island. Throughout the 1700s, the HBC was primarily interested in trading with Inuit for coastal products: sea mammals, baleen, ivory, blubber and oil (Graham 1969: 240-241; Robson 1759:63-66). As well, all trading was done at coastal locations where Inuit had summer camps for the purpose of hunting things from the ocean. Therefore, the value of trade goods was equal to a certain amount of coastal products in the absence of coinage. The segregation of trade goods as coastal products reiterates Igjugârjuk's view of trade goods; that they were very clever, often highly functional, but quite apart from Caribou Inuit culture.

An interesting element of Igjugârjuk's story of European origins is the relationship between the Europeans and Chipewyan. Though different than Europeans in purpose, they ultimately had the same origin, which was also incidental to the original existence of the Inuit. Although tensions between the two cultures may extend well into prehistory, the conflict between them in the 1700s is contextual to trade relations (Smith & Burch 1979: 78-81). The massacre at Knapp's Bay is an obvious example, where preferential treatment of the Inuit by the HBC was cited as a cause. As well, an important element of Hearne's narrative of the Bloody Falls massacre, however embellished, is the possibility that it was performed solely for the benefit of his witness (Beattie & Geiger 1993:157). Hearne records that after the attack, the Chipewyan destroyed all of the Inuit possession including perfectly good tents, tools, and large quantities of meat and fish. The only exception was European trade goods, which were pilfered (Hearne 1958:104). Rasmussen records several stories passed on through the Inuit, where Chipewyan were often attacked by Inuit for the purpose of taking their trade goods (Rasmussen 1930:102). This even includes a story entitled "Of the Days when one could get White Men's Goods by Murdering Indians". So the association of the Chipewyan with Europeans in Igjugârjuk's story is not without some historical merit. Inadvertent as it may have been, the presence of the HBC had social consequences for cross-cultural relations in the Kivalliq.

4.6 Summary of the Early Period of Trade 1717-1790

During the early period, particularly between 1750 and 1790, the Caribou Inuit could depend upon trade with the HBC which was brought to them (Burch 1986: 112; Fossett 2001: 92-113; Graham 1969:240-241; Robson 1759:66). The products purchased from the Inuit are consistent throughout the early trade period, including mostly blubber and oil from sea mammals, and occasionally walrus ivory and baleen from Bowhead whales. In spite of the discordance with the normal Caribou Inuit emphasis on caribou for subsistence, the trade pattern is not surprising. Once hunted and procured, these products could simply be picked up by the trade sloops with minimal transportation costs. The summer village sites would presumably have been occupied for that purpose, during that season, even if the traders had never made contact.

It is hard to quantify the impact on traditional life that the presence of HBC trade had upon the Inuit during this period, but an important observation is that the relationship between the two was generally one of subservience on the part of the HBC, who made all of the effort in travelling and bringing trade to the Inuit (see Figure 6). While there were material consequences upon the technology of the Inuit, it is difficult to know the extent to which this changed the base of the subsistence economy. It is possible that traditional migration patterns and schedules were not greatly affected at all as a result. By this, it is entirely feasible that rather than changing traditional life, trade goods initially supplemented it.

During the early period, there are both instances where the Caribou Inuit reacted to the HBC consistently as a group, and inconsistently as individuals. The acts of aggression towards the HBC by the different coastal communities in 1753 are a good example of a consensual response. In other cases however, the HBC, whilst struggling to make trades with the population in general, were successful in trading with individuals. It can be inferred that although there are general regional trends, along with specific unified reactions, the introduction of European trade did not affect all individuals equally, and in general the Inuit did not react in the same ways.

4.7 1790-1900 the Inuit Traders

Although a relationship of dependency may not have formed, European goods were not without value to the Caribou Inuit. Following the cessation of trade sloops in 1790, Caribou Inuit faced a dilemma if they wished to continue trade with the HBC; the tables were turned, and it was the Inuit who would have to make the arduous journey if European goods were valuable enough to them. It wasn't until 1861 that trade was again brought to the Inuit, initially by American whalers, and then by the HBC who eventually built a network of trade posts by the 1920s (Fossett 2001:176-177; Ross 1975; Williamson 1974: 69).

From the most southerly Inuit community at Knapp's Bay, the trip to Churchill is a minimum of 300 km, or a 600 km round trip (see Figure 1). The distance is even double that for the northernmost Caribou Inuit at the mouth of Chesterfield Inlet. The journey would also have been very dangerous (see Chapter 2). By winter, sudden blizzards would certainly have impeded any trip of such distance (Donald Uluadluak & Louie Angalik in Dawson et al. 2006: 120-122). In the spring and fall, erratic rains and river break-ups would have been very hazardous, creating the possibility of being stranded without shelter. Even in the summer, travel on the Bay would have been subject to sudden storms, strong currents, rocks, and large stretches of coast unsuitable for landing. Another complication would have been the transportation of goods intended for trade. Some items, such as ivory and baleen, which had been occasionally traded in the earlier period, would not have been too problematic. The bulk of Inuit trade, however, had been blubber and oil which would have been very difficult to transport in any quantity large enough to make the trip worthwhile (B.42/a/136a; Robson 1759: 66).

The difficult trip to Churchill would have also been problematic to schedule. Using the post-journals from the 1800s, along with diaries of various trips made by explorers such as Christian Leden, I would estimate that the trip to Churchill would have been a minimum of several weeks each way, depending on the location of departure (Leden 1990). The devotion of such a large amount of time would have been difficult when the traditional seasonal pattern of subsistence is considered. In the winter, when Caribou Inuit relied primarily on the yields of the fall caribou hunt, mobility would have been reduced by the need to stay close to the caches and stores from the previous season[22] (Bennett & Rowley 2004: 247; Stewart 1994: 30). The spring and early summer would also be challenging as these were periods of scarcity, when winter stores had been depleted, and caribou were difficult to hunt (Rasmussen 1930: 41-42). As well, any trip made during the summer would have to be carefully timed in order to ensure that the critical fall caribou hunt would not be missed, else they would be liable to starve in the winter. As a result, there does not seem to have been an ideal time to make such a protracted trip.

The consensual solution to this dilemma, on the part of the Caribou Inuit, seems to have been to ignore the change in European trade and continue to live traditionally; for most Caribou Inuit, European goods were not valuable enough to justify travelling to Churchill. From 1790 to the mid-1800s, Churchill only traded with 160 Inuit individuals, which includes several parties that travelled to Churchill from outside of the Caribou Inuit territory (Fossett 2001:163). Fossett estimates the population of the Kivalliq at around 800-1000 individuals in 1790, basing the number primarily on observations made by the HBC during the trade sloop years (Fossett 2001:112). This is probably a conservative estimate considering that the HBC only ever interacted with Inuit along the coast, not accounting for the possibility that much larger numbers were living inland. In either case, it would seem that the bulk of the Caribou

---

[22] See Chapter 5 for a detailed discussion of Caribou Inuit caching behaviour.

Inuit population continued their indifferent attitude towards HBC trade once it ceased to be brought to them. In terms of illustrative numbers, perhaps no more than 10% of the total Caribou Inuit population travelled to Churchill over a 60 year period after the trade sloops stopped their annual voyages in 1790. Indeed, well into the 1920s, there were Inuit living in the Kivalliq who had never seen a European, suggesting that they had never been to a trade post in their lifetime (Leden 1990: 261-264).

Absent from the written history, but perhaps most important to the regional economy of the period, are those Caribou Inuit who did not travel to Churchill. They formed the bulk of the population and were content to trade, yet unwilling to disrupt their lives to do so. The existence of such a population, lukewarm to European goods, provided a niche for entrepreneurial families to act as middlemen between the HBC and the general Caribou Inuit population. These Inuit acted as mediums by employing two different strategies to cope with the dilemma of travelling to Churchill.

1. Occasional Trade Journeys

After 1790, the Churchill post-journals are replete with reports of parties of Inuit who would show up to trade, and then leave immediately. The composition of these envoys was highly variable. In 1818 for example, 74 men showed up with a large quantity of furs (B.42/a/144). This appears to be the largest party ever to make the journey. On the other end of the spectrum, most parties included men and women in groups as small as 4 to 5 individuals. The trip to Churchill seems to have been made by such Inuit at fairly infrequent times; they did not travel every year, and some may have only made the trip once in their lifetime.

The arrival times of Inuit trade envoys at Churchill was usually very predictable. The peak of winter, in January and February, as well as early spring to mid-summer, were the most popular times. Inuit rarely travelled to the post in the fall, and there are only a couple of exceptions to this rule throughout the entire historic period. The locations from which such trips were made are quite diverse. Sometimes it is difficult to know where exactly Inuit were from, as they were simply described in post-journals by such terms as "Far-away Esquimaux" or "Strange Esquimaux". In the instances where their origins were recorded, it can be seen that Inuit were making the journey to Churchill from places as far away as Wager Inlet (see Figure 1) (see B.42/a/130, 135 & 192; Rae 1970:27). In general, Inuit trade parties were usually associated by Company staff with coastal locations. This is not surprising given the Company knowledge accumulated in the 1700s. However, by 1858, it was entirely clear to the HBC that many of the trading parties were actually travelling to Churchill from the interior of the Kivalliq, and that many of these Inuit lived the entire year inland (B.42/a/189a).

The strategy of making occasional trips to Churchill seems to have depended primarily on the accumulation of enough goods to make the trip worthwhile. These products usually included white and blue fox furs, wolverine furs, wolf furs, caribou parchments, sinew, seal skin boots, and occasionally caribou meat[23]. On good trips, fox furs could number around 400 and caribou parchments in the thousands (see B.42/a/132, 140). In those cases, it would seem that the Inuit traders had collected many more products than had been directly acquired by themselves. In these instances, it would seem that they were either representing, or conducting trade for their communities. Another possibility is that they had traded within their communities and made the trip for personal gain. The motives and incentives for those that made the journey probably involved a combination of these possibilities.

As the trips were infrequent, and carefully scheduled by those who made them, it would seem that they were still living fairly traditional lives. There is no evidence to suggest that any of them had replaced their primary occupation as Inuit hunters with their roles as long distance traders. By acting as middlemen, they also enabled the general Caribou Inuit population to carry on their traditional lives as well as access European products. There is however a subtle economic change; previously, Inuit had primarily traded coastal products with the HBC. The practicality of transportation and storage assigned a new value to the furs of animals that had not previously been economically important to the Caribou Inuit including foxes, wolverines, musk-ox, and wolves (see Harper 1964:13). It is difficult to assess the impact of this shift, but it can be noted that the bulk of furs transported to Churchill were white foxes, which would have been trapped during the winter (see B.42/a/191). Although furs were the most common items traded by Inuit during this period, the quantities are nowhere near the level that they reached in the 1900s once subsistence strategies had been dramatically altered around the maintenance of trap lines (Damas 1988; Williamson 1974).

2. The Incorporation of Long Distance Trade into Subsistence

A completely different strategy adopted by some Caribou Inuit was to significantly alter their subsistence pattern in order to incorporate the Churchill area, and therefore interact with the HBC on a much more intensive scale. Following the final trade sloop in 1791, 20 hunters along with their families arrived at Churchill in June. They traded a few furs which they had brought, and then proceeded to hunt seals at the mouth of the Churchill River (B.42/a/116). This was the start of a pattern which lasted until the 1870s. On most years, groups of Inuit would arrive at Churchill at variable times in the spring,

---

[23] Although small quantities of Caribou products had been traded as early as 1754 (see B.42/a/43), it wasn't until 1818-1819 (see B.42/a/144) that caribou products were traded in large quantities. It is unclear whether this shift reflects the demands of the HBC, or a change in the economic practices of the Inuit. This change coincides with a rumor in July of 1818 (B.42/a/144), that a Chipewyan party had been plundered by Inuit at an unknown inland location.

Caribou Inuit Traders of the Kivalliq

often with a large quantity of furs if it was a good year. They would trade immediately for provisions, such as ammunition and shot, and then proceed to the mouth of the Seal River some 40 km away (see Figure 1) (B.42/a/192). They would then spend a good deal of the summer hunting seals and whales, regularly bringing flensed portions of blubber to Churchill. The Seal River hunters would always leave by August in order to return to the North for the caribou hunt (B.42/a/116-192).

These Inuit became very familiar to the HBC who referred to them by a number of names, but most commonly as the "Homeguard Esquimaux" (Burch 1986:113). This term did not refer to a specific ethnic group as the Homeguards came from a variety of communities along the West coast of the Bay; specifically Knapp's Bay, Whale Cove, and some were possibly from as far away as Rankin Inlet (see Figure 6) (see Rae 1970:188-189).

In spite of their diverse associations, Inuit at the Seal River summer camp usually pooled their efforts, which can be seen in the collective purchasing of HBC whale boats in 1807 & 1821 (B.42/a/132 & 145). Notwithstanding their cooperation, there were occasionally internal disputes which might be related to their varied origins. In 1807, William Auld, who was the Post-master at the time, suggested that one of the reasons he sent workers to assist with the Seal River hunt was to keep the peace in order to ensure the steady flow of oil (B.42/a/132). Indeed, it can be observed that families would often arrive in waves, stretching from March to June, before heading to the river to hunt indicating that they were travelling from a number of different locations (see B.42/a/116-192). According to ethnographic maps of the 1920s, the Seal River Inuit probably included representatives from the Padlirmiut, Hauniqtormiut, and Qaernirmiut (see Figure 3).

The Seal River camp was very prosperous until about 1850. The population of Inuit who hunted there varied from year to year, invariably affecting the success of the hunt, but on some years the catch could number over 300 seals, and 92 belugas (see B. 42/a/132 & 185). There were a number of 'bad years' during this period where only a few families reached the post, but this seems to have been caused by poor travel conditions. The winter of 1843-1844 for example was a very bad year. It seems that the seal hunters had difficulty in returning to their own territory due to an early onset of winter. The hunters had to spend the winter scattered in small groups, the furthest only 9 days travel from Churchill (B.42/a/179). Relief had to be sent to those families from the post throughout the winter. Very few people came to the post during the following two years. Again in 1852, poor weather affected travel, but this time and early spring, preventing people from travelling to Churchill (B.42/a/186). It would seem that for the most part, Seal River Inuit had tended to arrive during the spring by sled, so that they could easily cross the rivers *en route*. They would then build kayaks near Seal River, where it was easy to procure wood, and use the boats to hunt seals and eventually return by water to the North (B.42./a/192).

As late as 1848, Inuit were able to conduct massive seal and beluga hunts about Seal River and Churchill (B.42/a/185). By 1853 however, the population of sea mammals seems to have been depleted to a critical level (B.42/a/186; Fossett 2001: 162). This is not surprising when it is considered that hundreds of animals were killed on some years by the Inuit alone (see B.42/a/132 & 185). The HBC was also conducting yearly whale hunts during this period as well. After the collapse of the seal and whale populations around Churchill, Inuit did still camp at Seal River and hunt, but without the same success as before (B.42/a/186-192). The era of the Seal River camp ended tragically in 1873, when sickness prevented the Inuit from hunting, and eventually all died over a 2 month period, having become too weak to travel north for the fall (B.42/a/192). This however, did not bring about the demise of the Homeguards, as the Company now referred to several of the Inland Inuit, who were certainly Ahiarmiut, as Homeguards as well (B.42/a/189a).

American Whalers: A New Venue for Trade

Simultaneous to the collapse of Seal River oil fishery was the introduction of trade from a new source. In 1860-61, two American whaling ships, *Northern Light* and *Syren Queen,* wintered to the north of Chesterfield, representing the expansion of American whaling in to Hudson Bay (see Figure 6) (Fossett 2001:176-177). News of this reached Churchill rapidly (B.42/a/190). The whalers, unlike the HBC who only ever employed one or two Inuit at a time, employed the Marble Islanders during the winter as hunters, and by summer as labourers and crews for the ships (Ross 1975:77-78). Women were also employed sewing and preparing skins for winter clothing (Ross 1975:77). The Whalers also had intensive interaction with Inuit to the North of Chesterfield Inlet, at Wager Bay and Aivilik (see Figure 3). By 1870, the whalers were heavily dependant on the Inuit for meat and provisions during the winter, and even began to trade for furs in order to supplement the whale hunt (Ross 1975:63-64).

The items traded by American whalers were more or less the same as those available from the HBC (see Ross 1975:69-70; Graham 1969:243, 314). They also traded whale boats which were used to travel as far south as Churchill in 1869 (B.42/a/191). Marble Island Inuit, who occasionally showed up at Churchill during the 1860s, reported that American visits were erratic, yet they wore American clothing, used American guns, and travelled with American boats (B.42/a/191-192). It seems feasible to suggest that the tragic events at Seal River in 1873 may be evidence that the Homeguards' position as middlemen for trade with communities to the North was usurped by the arrival of the whalers. The HBC, who saw the American Whalers as competition, resumed the trade sloops, and eventually opened a post at Chesterfield Inlet (B.42/e/11).

Figure 7 Central Arctic

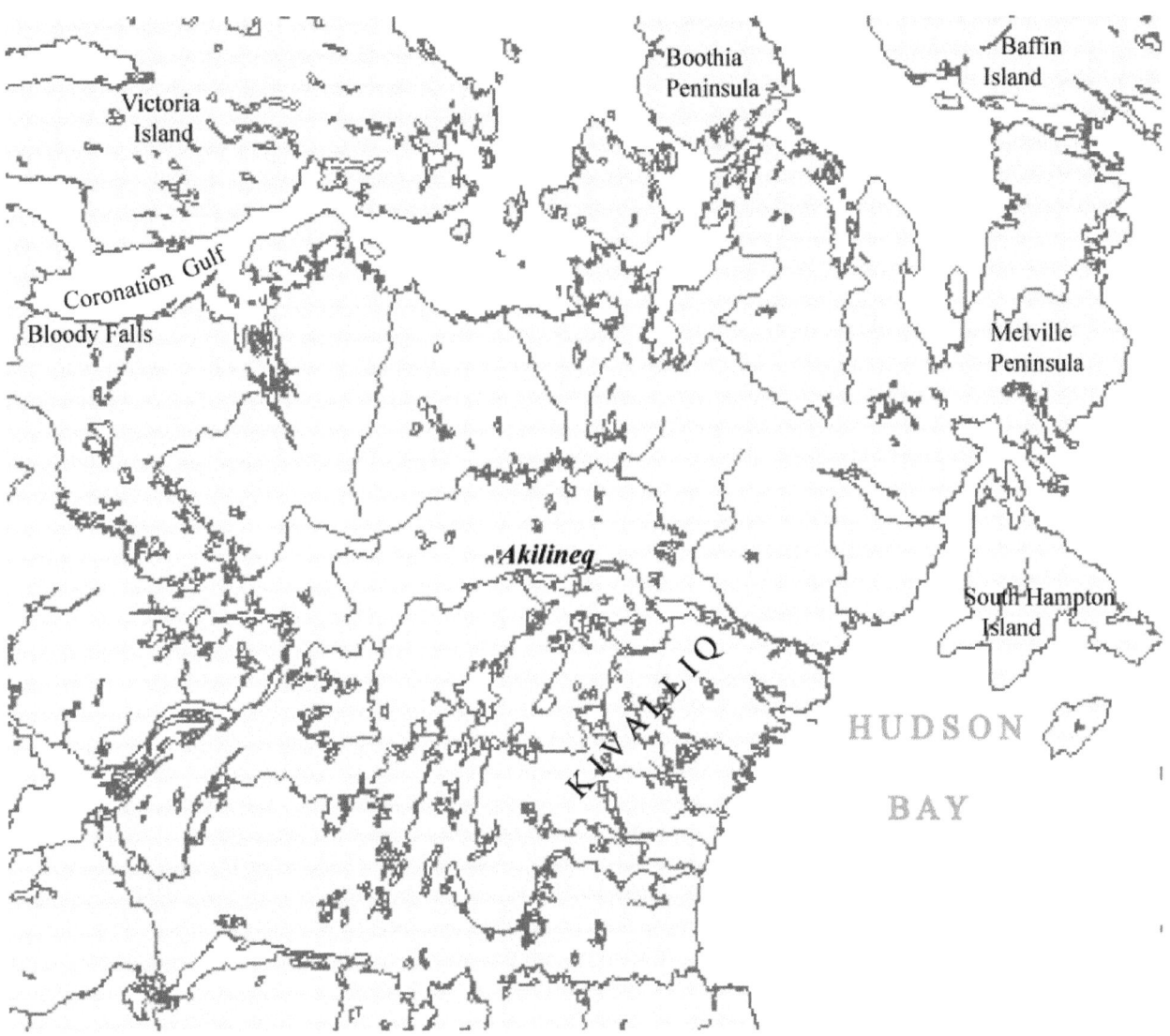

Homeguards and Long Distance Trade

Seal River and the incorporation of Churchill into subsistence was only one facet of Homeguard Inuit life; they were also involved in a long distance trade network with Inuit in the Kivalliq as well as more distant areas such as Coronation Gulf and the Melville Peninsula (see Figure 7). Long distance travel to locations where traditional Inuit met to trade seems to have been the definition of Homeguard life even at its inception. In 1815, for example, the Churchill post-master, Adam Snodie, was informed by the Seal River Inuit that they would not be returning the next year as they intended to travel to trade with "far-off tribes of Esquimaux" (B.42/a/142). He reiterated this in a letter to York Factory in 1818, suggesting that it was a normal pattern which most Seal River Inuit did regularly (B.42/a/142).

The Homeguard participation in regional trade was also noted by Rev. John West[24] in 1823, who was specific enough to suggest that there were locations at Chesterfield Inlet where Inuit would meet and trade European goods for traditional items such as sinew, fish hooks, and harpoons (Fossett 2001: 125). John Rae[25] echoed West in depicting the importance of traditional products being traded at Chesterfield (Rae 1866:139). An 1809 map drawn by an Inuk at Churchill also displays this division, with a small caption at Chesterfield Inlet that reads "Iskemos North of this point are not friendly with those that trade at Churchill[26]" (F.3/2 fo.9). The existence of an Inuit trade network was supported by observations made by other HBC staff right until 1913, when trade posts began to open into the interior

---

[24] Rev. John West, of the Anglican Church, visited Churchill in 1823 to assess the possibility of a mission (Fossett 2001:125).
[25] Dr. John Rae was an HBC explorer who passed through Kivalliq on expeditions in 1846 & 1851. Rae is most famous for finding relics that confirmed the demise of the Franklin Expedition (Rich 1953: lxvii-lxviii)
[26] The reference probably refers to the Aivilingmiut (F.3/2 fo.9)

(RG.3/20f/1/1). Even in 1922, Rasmussen wrote about *Akilineq*, which was a famous area where Inuit from all over the Kivalliq would meet to trade (Rasmussen 1930:27). *Akilineq* was located far inland, on the North shore of Aberdeen Lake (see Figure 7). Inuit from Churchill would meet there and trade with Copper Inuit, Netsilik and Utkusiksalingmiut. On Sir John Franklin's 1st Overland Expedition, he noted that Augustus, an Inuit HBC employee who was also a Seal River Homeguard, was well informed about the Inuit as far away as Wager Inlet to the North, and the Back River to the West, due to the fact that they regularly traded with them (see Figure 1) (Franklin 1823:264).

Rae, Snodie, and West are consistent in reporting that the Homeguards prevented other Inuit from travelling to Churchill, though they do not explain how this was accomplished (B.42/a/142 & 144; Fossett 2001: 125; Rae 1866:139). Rasmussen suggests that violent altercations occasionally happened at *Akilineq*, but these seemed to be more related to ethnic tensions rather than the trade (Rasmussen 1930:27). The suggestion that other Inuit were somehow deterred from travelling to Churchill is not consistent with the fact that at least some Inuit from the Kivalliq and beyond would indeed make occasional trips to Churchill as already discussed. One possibility is that Homeguards would attempt to meet such travellers, and trade with them before they reached Churchill, thus offering the incentive of shortening the trip.

There is some evidence to support the contention that the regional trade network may have actually preceded the existence of the Homeguards. In 1773, when Hearne encountered the Inuit at the Coppermine River, they were in possession of metallic trade goods which were almost certainly passed to them through Inuit hands (see Figure 7) (Hearne 1958: 104). An important possibility is that European goods and trade furs were not actually the foremost currency of the trade network even, in the 1800s. The products that were observed to be traded at *Akilineq* and Chesterfield included wood, sea mammal products, formed tools such as fish hooks and harpoons, sinew cordage, seal thongs, and lithic materials (Fossett 2001: 125; Rae 1866:39; Rasmussen 1930: 27). Trade relationships between communities could have been connected to kinship by marriage, which is a regional pattern that has been repeatedly noted by ethnographers (see Csonka 1994:32-34; Damas 1988:114; Williamson 1974:56-58). While European items may have been the cornerstone of the Homeguard economy, they may have just been one of many reasons why other Inuit travelled to such locations to trade. If traditional products and social relations were in fact the basis of Inuit markets, then it only seems natural that the Inuit trade network of the 1800s had its roots in prehistory; the network could indeed be a major factor in the very formation and development of Caribou Inuit culture in the first place.

4.8 Profiles of Caribou Inuit Traders

For the Homeguards, European trade was the basis of their economic lives. They specialized as intermediaries who transported things procured by the Inuit to Churchill, and European goods from Churchill to the Inuit. On the surface, this would seem to be a radical shift, dividing the Homeguards from Caribou Inuit that were living a more traditional subsistence at the time; indeed, the evidence would suggest that this pattern demanded journeys of extraordinary distance. However, the Homeguards retained their ethnic identities, and still participated socially and ideologically in Inuit culture. Using historical records, along with oral tradition, it is helpful to examine the profiles of several individuals, and groups of individuals, that were considered Homeguards. Of specific interest is the manner in which their role as middlemen set them apart from other Caribou Inuit, but also the ways in which they functioned as members of that society.

Ullebuk (Ullebuk Sr.)

Ullebuk was a Padlirmiut Homeguard and one of the first Inuit to actually be employed by the HBC. As an employee, he travelled extensively with various HBC expeditions, to the point that he was probably one of the most well-travelled Arctic explorers of his day (Rich 1953:370). At a point in time where many Caribou Inuit would not even travel to Churchill, Ullebuk became a distinguished individual in the HBC, and was quite wealthy by European standards. Ullebuk was simultaneously a prominent member of Inuit society; he had a large family, and is the direct ancestor of many Padlirmiut that live in the community of Arviat today (Lyons 2007: 15-16).

Ullebuk was first employed by the HBC as a second Inuit hand to accompany Sir John Franklin's 2nd Overland Expedition in 1824 (Rich 1953:370). On that trip, he ended up spending most of his time surveying the Coppermine and Mackenzie Rivers. Although he spoke little English at the time, he was invaluable to the expedition in forming relationships with the new Inuit groups that the explorers encountered. Ullebuk was described as an extremely loyal, good worker, and was excellent in temper (Franklin 1828). Returning to Churchill in 1827, he spent most of his time around the post until he was officially employed in 1829. Robert Harding, the post-master at the time, frequently mentions the whereabouts and activities of Ullebuk, often commenting on how he was an integral member of the post-staff (B.42/a/155).

In 1829, Ullebuk was sent on another expedition with another older Inuk named Moses, but this time to Ungava in Northern Quebec (B.42/a/155; Rich 1953:371). Again, Ullebuk was instrumental in the success of that expedition, and was held at Fort Chimo for six years where he acted as an interpreter and hunter. Ullebuk's time in Quebec seems to have been highly lucrative, and he began to save money. In 1837, he left

Fort Chimo, and over the next 6 years spent time at a variety of posts. He did some more expedition work, travelling from the Mackenzie Region to Boothia Peninsula in 1839 with Dease and Simpson, before arriving at York Factory, on James Bay, in 1843 with his family (Rich 1953: 371). Ullebuk and his family were described by the York Factory Post Officer's wife, Letitia Hargrave, in a gossipy letter to a friend in England. According to Mrs. Hargrave, Ullebuk had managed to save over £100 which would have been a very large sum for an Inuk in the 1800s. He had with him an attractive wife, a 12-year old son, and a younger daughter (Rich 1953:371). Ullebuk then travelled with Dr. John Rae on his mapping expedition of 1846-47, accompanied by his son William Ullebuk (Rae 1970). After 1847, the Ullebuks returned to the Kivalliq and lived among the Inuit again, visiting Churchill occasionally until Ullebuk Sr.'s death in 1852 (see Rich 1953:371).

William Ullebuk (Ullebuk Jr.)

William Ullebuk is perhaps the most principal Inuit figure in the history of HBC trade in the Kivalliq; he is certainly the individual with the most recorded about him, and he still figures prominently in the social memory of the Padlirmiut community (Donald Uluadluak in Lyons 2007: 15). His exact date of birth is unknown, but he was described as being about 12 years of age by Letitia Hargrave, in 1843; this would place William's birth around 1831, when his father was working at Fort Chimo in Ungava. Hargrave described him as a clever boy who, although a bit mischievous, could speak ten languages. At the very least, these languages included Inuktitut, English, Cree, Dene, French, and presumably some other Native languages from his time in Ungava (see Rich 1953: 371).

William Ullebuk became very familiar with John Rae; on his 1846-47 expedition to map and explore Repulse Bay and the coast of the Melville Peninsula, William Ullebuk often acted as an interpreter when his father was otherwise occupied (see Figure 7) (Rae 1970). This made William familiar with the geography and people of the entire coast of Hudson Bay at a very early age. He had not previously lived in the Kivalliq, even though his father was a prominent figure in the area.

Between 1847 and 1850, William resided somewhere in the Kivalliq, living with his Caribou Inuit family that he had not previously known (Rich 1953: 373). In 1850, he visited Churchill with his father, and the Post-master attempted to coerce him to work there permanently as a translator. William had recently been married however, and he returned to the Kivalliq with his father (B.42/a/185).

Ullebuk Sr. died in 1852, and as Dr. John Rae was mounting an expedition to map the Boothia Peninsula, William was taken along in his father's capacity (Rae 1953:256). His salary as a member of the expedition was £20, but as the expedition discovered the fate of Franklin, he shared in the reward and profited a further £210 (Rich 1953: 373). There appears to have been some personality issues between Rae and William. Rae often chastised William in his various letters and diaries, lamenting his father and suggesting that William was not as useful (see Rae 1953: 239). At one point, in 1854, Rae reports that William attempted to abandon the expedition to join other Inuit (Rae 1953: 274). In other entries, Rae is highly appreciative of William. Upon parting ways in 1854, he presented William with an exquisite hunting knife that had been passed to him by Sir George Back, who had intended the knife to be passed to Ullebuk Sr. in commemoration of the Back River survey (Rae 1953: 285).

William, who must have been very wealthy even by European standards, worked for the company intermittently after travelling with Rae. Between 1855 and 1861, he worked for the Company at Churchill acting as an interpreter and middleman for the Inuit trade, and as a hunter to procure food for the Post (B.42/a/187-188, 189a, 190). William was the Company's first choice to accompany the Anderson and Stewart[27] expedition in 1855, but appears to have made himself scarce to avoid going (Barr 1999: 44, 69) After he left regular employment in 1861, he frequented the post on a nearly annual basis, always in association with the Seal River Homeguards (B.42/a/190-192). A good number of those Homeguards died during 1873, with William bearing witness to several of their deaths (B.42/a/192). He worked for the company again until 1874, even though barely any Inuit visited Churchill during that year (B.42/a/192). After 1874, he was not officially engaged by the company, but he appears to have been making some very large personal journeys promoting their trade. For example, in July of 1875, he left Churchill with a group of Marble Island Inuit who had made a rare journey to Churchill. Nothing was seen of him until March of 1877 when he arrived by sled with a group of Ahiarmiut from the interior (B.42/a/192). It would seem that his itinerary during those years would have been to travel as far as Marble Island, where he worked for the American Whalers for a period and likely wintered there (Fossett 2001: 271). At some point, he must have travelled inland via Chesterfield Inlet, perhaps as far as *Akilineq* to trade, and then travelled down the Kazan river, through Hikoligjuaq Lake before travelling overland to Churchill with the Ahiarmiut.

In 1878, William Ullebuk was able to purchase a small schooner which he used to transport goods and people up and down the coast from as far away as Wager Inlet, down to Churchill (Fossett 2001: 271). By this point in time, William was clearly an independent trader of prominence; he was very well known in the Kivalliq and was referred to by the Caribou Inuit as *Ihumatayualak* which meant "Little Big Boss" (Donald

---

[27] At the request of the British Admiralty, the HBC sent James Anderson and James Stewart to follow up on the evidence of Franklin's fate which had been discovered by Rae and William Ullebuk in 1854. The expedition was mounted by canoe, and travelled down Back's River to the Arctic Coast (Barr 1999).

Caribou Inuit Traders of the Kivalliq

Uluadluak in Lyons 2007:15). He then returned to the HBC in 1882, when he was employed as a trader and harpooner on their whaling ships which travelled as far as Marble Island before retiring in 1894. He died the winter of the following year (Rich 1953: 373-374).

The Coastal Homeguards

During the 1860-70s, the Inuit described by the Company as "Coastal Homeguards" were having a very rough time due to the collapse of the Seal River oil fishery, in contrast to the affluence they had experienced between 1790-1850 (B.42/a/144-192). Their trade during this period was often described as pitiful, and infrequent. A major part of the problem seems to have been that the Seal River had been over fished, and Homeguards could not bring in the same number of animals that they had been able to during the earlier years (B.42/a/190 & 191).

Several of the Homeguards at this time were referred to by name at Churchill Post as leaders of distinct bands including: Wot-Wot, Kyake, Old Kombeck, The Little Chief, and Taliak – the Little Chief's brother (B.42/a/190-192). These individuals were usually named in association with each other, as well as William Ullebuk. When presented with the names that they are referred to in the HBC archives, the Padlirmiut Elders at Arviat were not able to recognize any of them with the exception of Taliak (Lyons 2007:15). 'Taliak' was probably the name that the HBC staff used to refer to and individual named Talirituq, whom the Elders associated with the Qaernermiut at Chesterfield Inlet (see Figure 3). Talirituq's name meant 'with big arms' and he was a famous *Angakok* (shaman) renowned for his special out-of-body ability (Lyons 2007: 15).

Although usually mentioned in association with each other, each of these individuals seems to have been fairly independent, and would often arrive at Seal River at different times. In 1871 for example, Wot-Wot arrived on March the 2nd, The Little Chief on May 13, and Old Kombeck and his band, numbering 28, on May 30 bringing news that Taliak would also be coming with his band as well (B.42/a/192). Those who arrived early by sled seem to have spent time building kayaks before the ice broke up, but the Seal River hunters also owned several whale boats, which they used as well. They would always leave by the beginning of August for their own country in order to hunt Caribou, but they were certainly involved in larger trading networks during the winter because they would usually arrive with very large quantities of furs to trade (B.42/a/190-192).

Most of the Coastal Homeguards died during a particularly tragic year, 1873, when a series of unfortunate events coincided with an epidemic and a poor Seal hunt. When the first of the Coastal Homeguards arrived in March, they were low on provisions and had little to exchange, indicating that it had also been a poor year for trade during the winter. Over the course of the summer, the Seal River camp was struck with influenza, and as many as fourteen of the thirty men at the camp died, leaving the rest in a state of starvation (B.42/a/192; Fossett 2001:179). At the beginning of August, Wot-Wot, the Little Chief, and Taliak set off with what remained of their families, and nothing more was heard until William Ullebuk showed up in Churchill on August 28th. He had set off with a party of eight from a community North of Whale cove by kayak. It is uncertain what he would have been doing travelling this late in the season given that ice would have already started to form on the Bay, but considering the timing of the Coastal Homeguards departure from Churchill, it seems likely that William had been out looking for them as they hadn't arrived in the North. The eight men that William was with had lashed their kayaks together and formed a sail of caribou skin, whilst he paddled alongside. A sudden squall hit, and the eight men were unable to get the sail down in time and were all drowned, with William Ullebuk being the only survivor. He continued the journey and eventually ran into the Little Chief. His brother Taliak had died along with his wife and his son. The Little Chief himself and the rest of the survivors were in a very bad state, lying on the beach perfectly helpless and dying; they were too sick to hunt. Unable to help, William left them and continued to Churchill, and soon stumbled upon Wot-Wot and his band in a similar state. Wot-Wot's body was later found in October. At the end of the year, the Post-master's final entry declared it the worst year in their history, saying that out of thirty, only five Coastal Homeguards remained (B.42/a/192).

Though it was ultimately disease and misfortune at the core of the disaster, it had been a particularly bad year in terms of trade and hunting as well. The Coastal Homeguards hadn't really been able to bring any trade goods to the post in the first place, and then the Seal River hunt had been a disaster (B.42/a/192). Their long-distance trade network had probably recently collapsed. The Ahiarmiut who lived inland and to the west no longer depended upon the Coastal Homeguards, as a few had themselves become Homeguards and were making trips

Table 6 Contents of an 1864 Ahiarmiut Trade at Churchill Post (B.42/a/191)

Items	Quantity
White Fox	367
Blue Fox	2
Wolves	18
Wolverine	3
Caribou Parchment	1768
Fish (whole)	36
Arctic Hares (whole)	5
Caribou Meat	2000 lbs
Caribou Heart	57
Caribou Tongue	56
Grease	419 lbs
Sinew	18 lbs
Seal Skin Line	56 lbs

Figure 8 H.H. Hall's Map (Adapted from RG.3/20f/1/1 by H.H. Hall 1913)

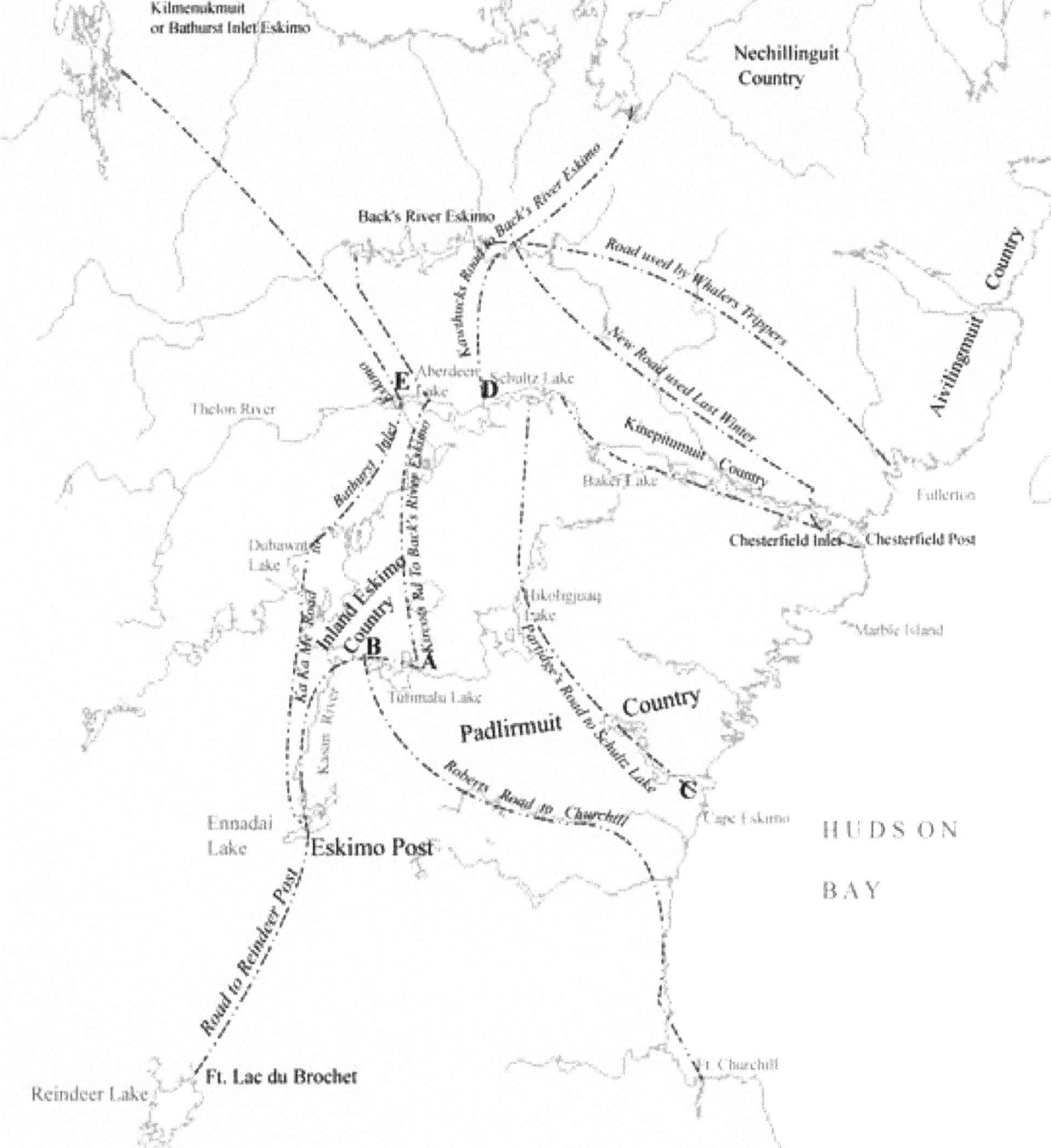

A - Kircot's Camp   B - Robert's Camp   C - Partridge's Camp   D - Kawthuck's Camp   E - *Akillineq*

to both Churchill and the Lac du Brochet trade post, in Northern Saskatchewan (B.42/a/189a). The Ahiarmiut Homeguards seem to have been making covert trades at Churchill as early as the 1850s (see Figure 3). Between 1850 and 1870, a curious pattern was that they would show up in the dead of winter, and place their sleds and camps behind rocks as though they were hiding. They would trade the next day and then leave immediately (B.42/a/189a-192). Although it is difficult to place their motives, it may be possible that they were trying to avoid being seen by the Coastal Homeguards. Another interesting element of the winter trade is that a number of coastal products were also being traded by the Ahiarmiut as well, including ivory, seal skin boots, and seal skin line. Consider, for example, the contents of a trade made on February 27th 1864 with 4 Inland Inuit, presumably Ahiarmiut, who had arrived by sled and hid behind a rock outcrop near to Churchill (see Table 6). It later became apparent that the Ahiarmiut were acting as intermediaries for the Inuit as far away as the Arctic coast, and by doing so, may have usurped Coastal Homeguards control over trade centres such as *Akilineq* (Csonka 1994).

Figure 9 Donald Uluadluak's Drawing of Qiqut (Uluadluak in Lyons 2007)

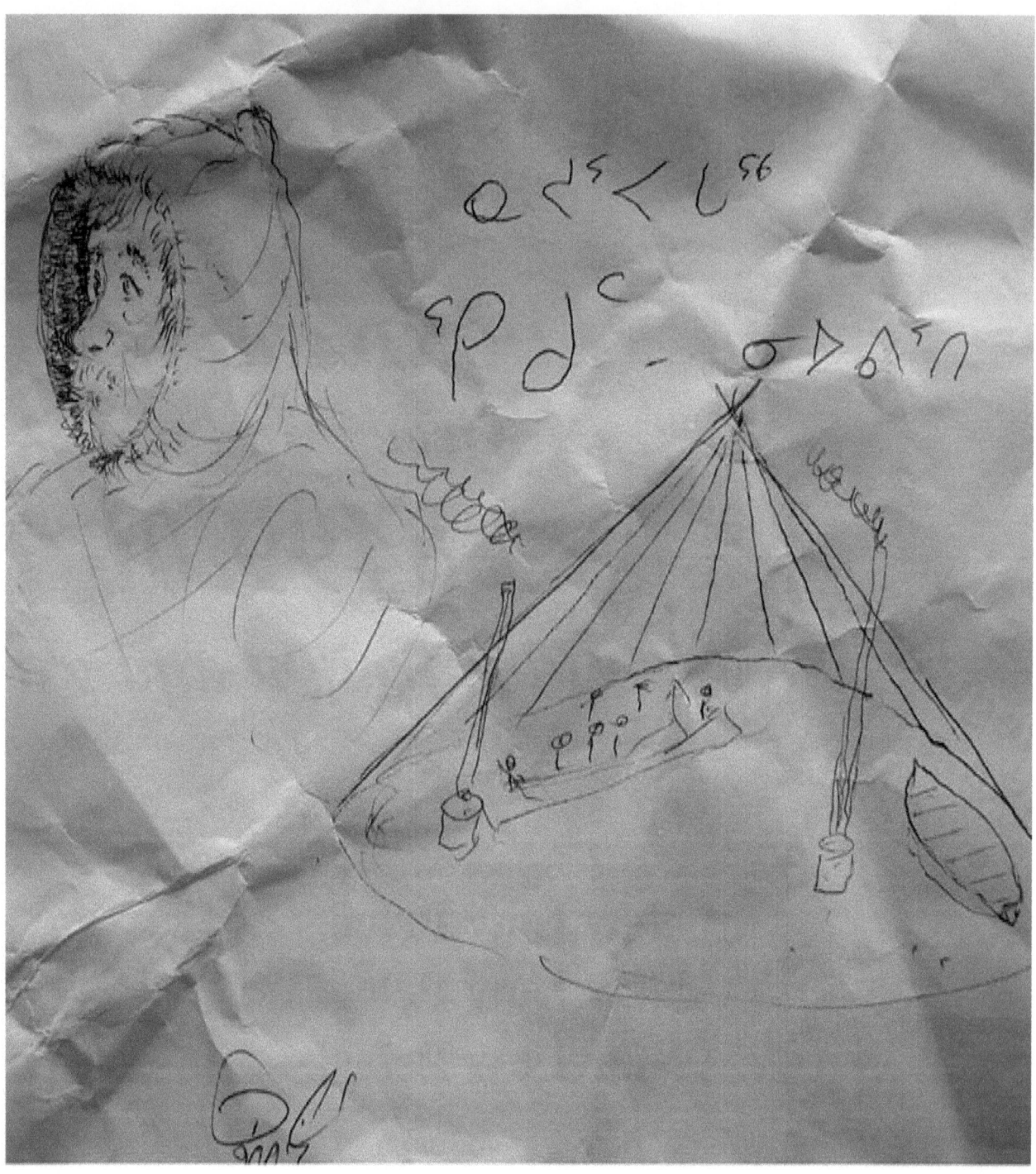

The presence of American Whalers after 1861 probably circumvented the Coastal Homeguard trade relations as well. When Inuit from Marble Island visited the post during the 1860s, they wore American clothing, and travelled in American whale boats- a good indication that the Americans were now their primary source for trade goods, rather than the Chesterfield centres mentioned by Rae and West in the 1840s (B.42/a/192). After the tragic events of 1873, there were very few Coastal Homeguards with the exception of William Ullebuk. By the time populations rebounded, after 1900, there was a series of trade posts that had been set up distributing their monopoly on European trade even further (RG.3/20/F/1/1).

The Ahiarmiut Traders

The Ahiarmiut are a sub-group of the Caribou Inuit, who traditionally lived the entire year on the lakes and rivers to the South and West of Hikoligjuaq Lake (see Figure 3). Ahiarmiut traders, referred to as "Inland

Esquimaux" in the post-journals[28], were making occasional trips to Churchill by 1858, and a number were considered Homeguards by the 1870s (B.42/a/189a & 192). Ahiarmiut traders always arrived at Churchill during the winter and travelled by sled. Initially, the Ahiarmiut traded at Churchill exclusively, but by 1868, some also travelled to the Lac Du Brochet HBC post at Reindeer Lake, Saskatchewan (see Figure 1)(Barr 1991: 23; Fossett 2001:181).

In a letter written in 1913 by H.H. Hall[29], the Ahiarmiut are described as being at the centre of a large regional network that stretched from Churchill to Bathurst Inlet (RG.3/20F/1/1). A map that accompanied the letter identifies two Ahiarmiut individuals, Qaqami and Qiqut (spelled KaKaMe and Kircot on the map), including the routes that they travelled, and the locations of their camps (Figure 8).

Qaqami was the wealthiest of the Ahiarmiut traders, and an extraordinary traveller who made several journeys from Reindeer Lake to Bathurst Inlet, and possibly the Coppermine River – a minimum of 1500 km each way (see Figure 1 & 5) (Csonka 1994:33-34; Jenness 1922:49; Rasmussen 1932: 67-71). Qaqami was encountered by the ethnographer Diamond Jenness during his visit with the Copper Inuit in the Coronation Gulf in 1915 (Jenness 1922). Qaqami traded ammunition, knives, snow knives, and saws to the Copper Inuit who did not personally travel into the Kivalliq further than *Akilineq*. Qaqami had a large family with many children, and as many as 3 wives at one point (Jenness 1922: 49).

Qiqut is particularly interesting as Padlirmiut Elders in Arviat remember a great deal about him (Donald Uluadluak in Lyons 2007: 37-38). Donald Uluadluak was even able to draw a picture of him based on descriptions that had had heard (Figure 9). Qiqut travelled regularly to Churchill and Reindeer Lake, bringing European goods back to a camp that he operated at east side of the Kazan River. He also seems to have made occasional trips to the Utkhusiksalingmiut at Back River by way of *Akilineq* (Figure 7&8).

Qiqut is best remembered by the Padlirmiut Elders for the permanent tent from which he conducted his business. His tent was located on the east side of Tulimalu Lake on the Kazan River, and he would invite local Ahiarmiut, and possibly Chipewyan to trade there at all times of the year (Figure 8). Qiqut's tent was so large that it had two stoves, and he not only kept his trade goods inside, but also his kayak (see Figure 9) (Donald Uluadluak in Lyons 2007:37-38). Donald Uluadluak's drawing depicts a circular tent, with two pipe-chimneys over the stoves. The use of winter tents with pipe-stove chimneys was practiced by the Ahiarmiut even until the 1960s (see Plate 9). Qiqut's tent served as a location where he conducted local trades, and had a very similar function to the HBC trade posts themselves. Local Ahiarmiut, who didn't want to travel to Churchill could simply go to Qiqut's tent.

The Ahiarmiut trader's involvement with the Company coincided with the 'Musk-ox Boom', which started around 1860. Musk-ox prices soared to $24.53, per fur, by 1888, and briefly became the HBC's primary source of income in the North; this lead to the rapid depletion of musk-ox herds (Barr 1991: 23, 44-47, 63-54). The musk-ox became so rare that the Canadian government tried to protect them by places hunting restrictions in 1894, and again in 1917 (Barr 1991: 42-43). These laws, which were to be enforced by the Royal Northwest Mounted Police, brought the Inuit of the Kivalliq into contact with a governing authority for the first time (see Rasmussen 1930: 32). A very large portion of Ahiarmiut trade included musk-ox during the 1880s. This may partially explain the reason that the Ahiarmiut trade network covered such a large area; as the musk-ox became more dispersed, they had to travel larger distances to procure them. However, the locations of *Akilineq* and the Thelon River as centres of regional Inuit trade and interaction appear to predate

4.9 Discussion

Company economics assigned different values to Inuit products than the Inuit economy did. In order to act as intermediaries between the HBC and the Inuit, the Homeguards had to negotiate both economies. Churchill was a fixed location that could be accessed all year. Other than variability in the world market, which controlled Company prices, Churchill was a stable and reliable resource to the Homeguards. However, the Inuit with which the Homeguards traded were not fixed to locations, nor would they have been able to trade in all seasons. Furthermore, success in procuring furs for trade would have been highly variable between years due to the volatile nature of the Kivalliq. As a result, the Caribou Inuit themselves were the major factor in the Homeguard economy. The Homeguards had to travel great distances to Inuit trade centres, maintain semi-permanent camps at major cross roads, and incorporate new technologies such as whaleboats and schooners to transport goods.

The changes made by Homeguards in order to act as middlemen were dramatic, yet it is apparent from the profiles of such Inuit traders that the social and ideological world in which they existed was Inuit. They retained their ethnic memberships, and were still

---

[28] Burch uses the appearance of the 'Inland Esquimaux' in the Churchill Post Journals to support his theory that it wasn't until the mid-1800s that Caribou Inuit began to live the entire year in the interior of the Kivalliq (Burch 1986:113-114). This would represent the genesis of the Ahiarmiut as a distinct cultural entity in the Kivalliq. In this model, the term 'Ahiarmiut', which means 'those who live separately', may not have existed in that time period (see Csonka 1994: 34). However, when presented with the names of 'Inland Esquimaux', Padlirmiut Elders identify them as direct ancestors of those who currently identify themselves as Ahiarmiut (Lyons 2007).

[29] H.H. Hall was an HBC Employee who traveled in the interior of the Kivalliq in the early 1900s to investigate possible locations for future trade posts. Hall's mission was specifically motivated by the desire to re-route Inuit traders in order to cut-off interaction with American whalers, who the HBC saw as competition at the time (RG.3/20f/1/1).

connected to their communities through kinship and marriage. They travelled with their extended families. Homeguards were also hunters themselves and conducted their trade through traditional venues. Because the Caribou Inuit world view associated European items with the Ocean, Homeguards would have necessarily been participants in the ideology as well; they would have almost certainly been amulet holders in order to negotiate the strict taboos and protocols regarding the items that they traded (see Rasmussen 1930: 34, 48). The Homeguards were able to completely reorder their mode of production, yet they remained culturally traditional.

Continuity of Historical Bias in Profiles?

The profiling of specific individuals has been made possible because of their prominence in the historical records created by the HBC and various explorers. From that point of view, it would seem that the Inuit traders discussed were the instigators of economic change in the Caribou Inuit population during the historic period before 1900. The HBC was not successful at integrating European trade into Caribou Inuit subsistence during the period of 1717-1790. Ultimately, it was Inuit traders who incorporated European technologies, by making them available in terms of the existent subsistence patterns and social networks.

In this view, Inuit traders were entrepreneurial individuals who were the primary agents of social change in their culture during the historic period. This in itself is an advancement of models concerning the cultural transition of Caribou Inuit peoples during the colonial period. Rather than a homogenous cultural entity reacting and adapting to an external force, the agency of individuals in shaping the process is considered. There is, however, a discrepancy with ethnographic knowledge regarding the political process in Caribou Inuit society. The concepts of leadership and decision making in Caribou Inuit society have previously been discussed in Chapter 3. Family solidarity was the most important element of action. Rather than having decisions made by an autocratic patriarch, open committee and discussion were constantly in process to achieve family consensus. R.G. Williamson has suggested that individual leadership has often been assumed by anthropologists in cases where individuals were merely acting as spokespersons to articulate family consensus. Particularly in the case of European interaction, the individual chosen to represent the family was often a middle-aged male with physical prowess; such an individual was more likely to be taken seriously (Williamson 1974: 41-42).

It is very rare in the historical documentation of the era that the families of Caribou Inuit males who traded at Churchill were ever mentioned, yet there is little doubt that they were present. One of the instances where families are mentioned is the very first year that Caribou Inuit travelled to Churchill in 1791, immediately following the cessation of the trade sloops. It was recorded that 20 hunters along with their families arrived at Churchill and spent the summer hunting seals in the vicinity (B.42/a/116). In traditional life, survival demanded the cooperation of the extended family; it was the unit through which labour was organized to ensure successful hunting, maintenance of equipment, and stockpiling of supplies. Homeguard life may not have been too different in that respect. The Seal River oil fishery is an excellent example, where the success of the hunt would have relied on more than the action of men using their kayaks to spear seals. Clothes, tents, and kayaks still had to be sewn, blubber had to be processed, meat prepared and cured, etc.

Prominence of individuals in the eyes of the HBC traders and explorers cannot be equated to prominence of individuals in Caribou Inuit society. It seems unlikely that the concept of leadership and decision making was any different in a Homeguard family than it would have been for a family that opted to not travel to Churchill. The decisions to incorporate Churchill into subsistence, travel long distances, and trade amongst other Caribou Inuit, probably represent more than the intentions of any particular individual. So the historical data is significantly biased because it rarely reports the whereabouts and activities of the extended families that the individuals who have been profiled were related to. In this context, an archaeological example is of use because it offers the chance to study material patterns that were created by the activities of more than one individual.

Chapter 5 – Archaeology of House I

5.1 Introduction

The objective of this study is to look at the ways that the Caribou Inuit themselves incorporated European goods and technologies into their society. At this point, it has been concluded that the primary agents of that process were Inuit traders referred to as 'Homeguards'. Previously, in Chapter 4, the profiling of specific Homeguards was made possible by their prominence in historical documentation. However, it has also been pointed out that such a depiction is biased by the perspectives of the HBC post-staff and explorers who recorded the information in the first place. Aside from cultural dispositions, geography is another major source of bias which must be considered; HBC staff, in general, made all of their observations of Caribou Inuit traders at Churchill, Manitoba during very short trade encounters - very little can be surmised about their lives beyond the view of Fort Prince of Wales as a result. Archaeology then is a powerful approach to this problem because there is a high potential that Caribou Inuit traders left material evidence at Kivalliq archaeological sites that were formed in the 1800s.

Chapter 5 is an archaeological examination of a large house pit, referred to as House I, which was excavated at the *Ihatik* site on Austin Island, Nunavut (Figure 10). The analysis reveals that House I is remarkably different from typical Caribou Inuit structures, and that it dates to the mid/late-1800s. Historically, this is a significant time period because Inuit traders, known as Homeguards, were the primary link between the Caribou Inuit, and the HBC at Churchill (see Chapter 4).

Figure 10 Austin Island, Nunavut

Table 7 Quantities of Feature Types at the *Ihatik* Site (JhKl – 1 & 2)

Feature Description	Total
Grave	5
Cache	46
Cache (pit variety)	20
Cairn	9
Fox Trap	2
Hearth	1
House (semi-subterranean)	1
Hunting Blind	1
Kayak Stand	12
Tent Rings	
Single	70
Bilobate	2
Semi-subterranean	3
Toy	6
Grand Total	178

The *Ihatik* site, which includes both JhKl-1 and JhKl-2[30], is a series of archaeological features on a terrace that is 20m above Maguse Point, which stretches out into Hudson Bay (Figure 11). The site was studied by Dr. Peter Dawson during the summer of 2006, and includes over 178 features including various tent rings, caches, kayak stands, fox traps, hunting blinds, graves, and surface middens (see Table 7) (Dawson et al. 2007). All of the features were mapped and surface collections of associated artifacts and faunal materials were taken as well. In addition, 2 structures were excavated; the large house pit in question and a single tent ring.

Other than House I, the archaeological pattern at *Ihatik* generally conforms to that of other coastal archaeological sites in the vicinity of Arviat, including *Qikiktarrjuk*, Sentry Island (*Arviaq*), and *Nuvuq* Point (Figure 10) (Bertulli 1989, Dawson 2005; Dawson et al. 2007). Such sites seem to have served as locations for summer aggregations of Padlirmiut as described in Birket-Smith's (1929a) ethnography (see also Lyons 2007:36). Travelling down the Maguse River, Padlirmiut would arrive in the vicinity of Arviat early in the spring to hunt seals spending the summer in large groups, and living in small conical tents. They would return inland at

---
[30] JhKl-1 and JhKl-2 are official site names designated by the Canadian Borden system.

Caribou Inuit Traders of the Kivalliq
Figure 11 Map of the Ihatik Site (JhKl 1 & 2)

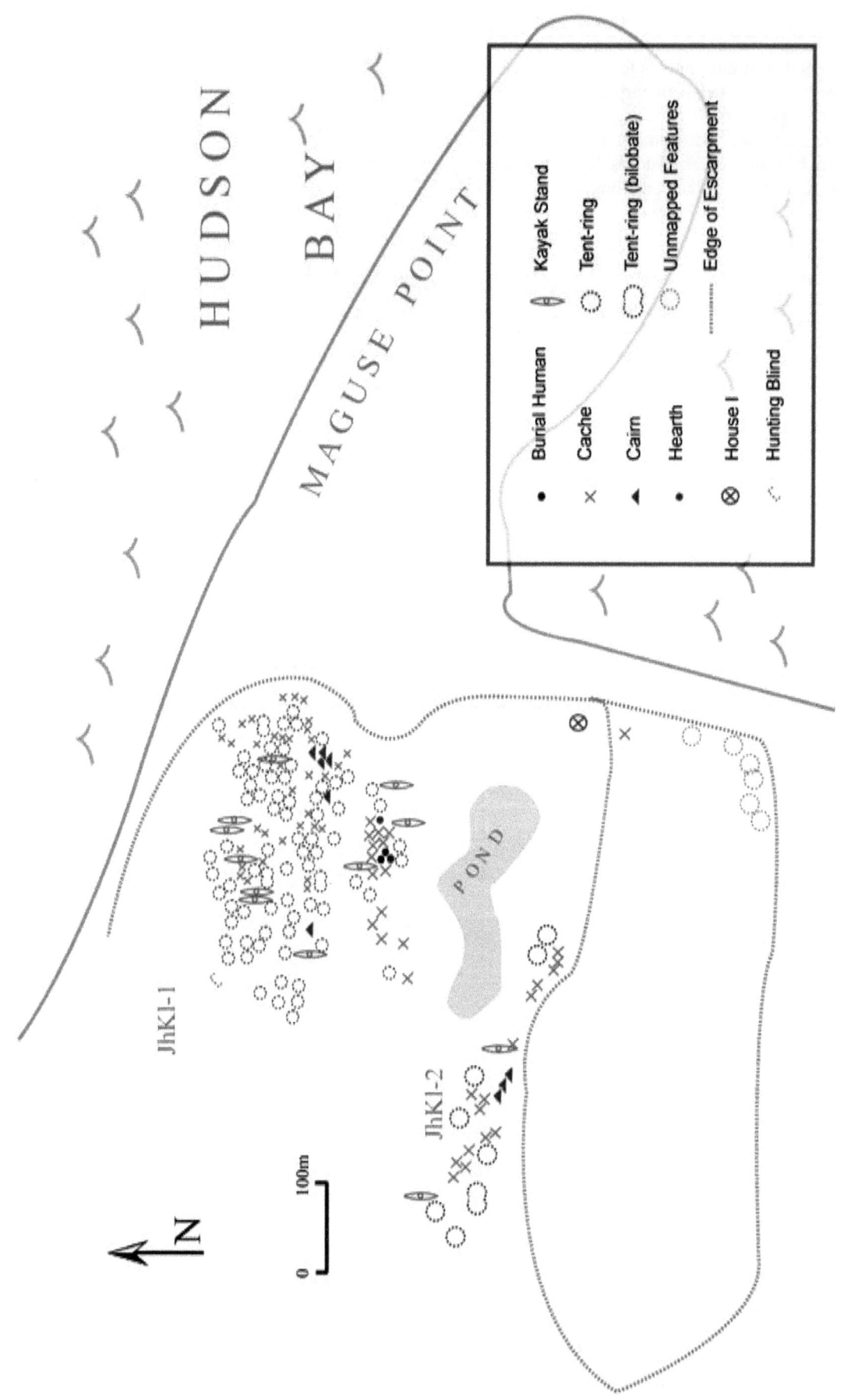

Chapter 5 – Archaeology of House I

Figure 12 House I Photos

View facing Northwest (photo credit Peter Dawson 2006)

View facing South with edge of escarpment highlighted.
Note Sentry Island (*Arviaq*) on the horizon. (photo credit Peter Dawson 2006)

Figure 12 House I Photos

View facing West. Note pit-cache feature built into the edge of the escarpment (photo credit Peter Dawson 2006)

View facing South after excavation

Chapter 5 – Archaeology of House I

Figure 13 House I Local Topography

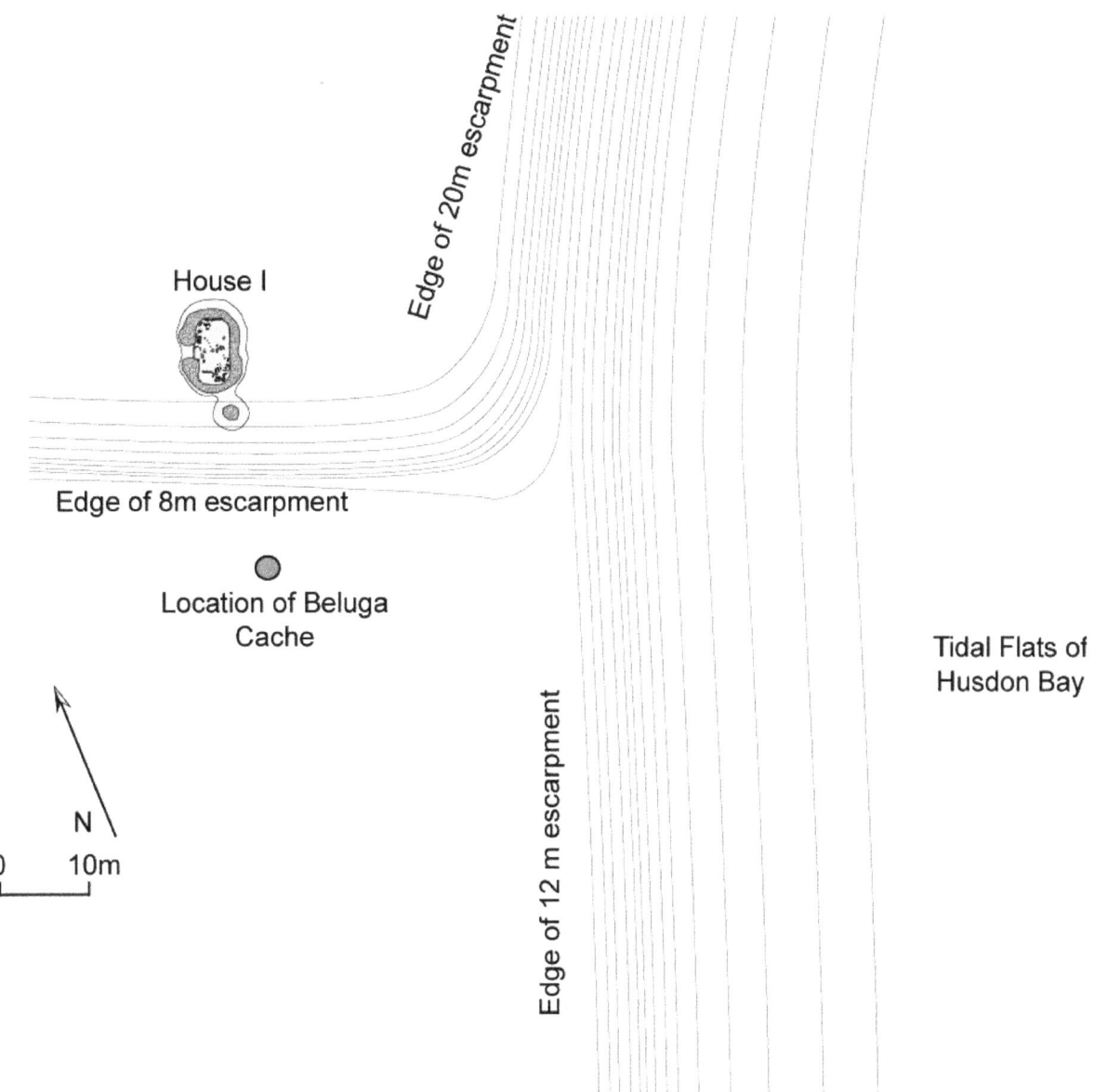

the onset of September in order to intercept the fall caribou migration and spend the winter at inland locations such as Hikoligjuaq Lake (see Figure 1) (see Chapter 3). '*Ihatik*' is an Inuktitut word used to describe something that stretches out like an arm, and is a common name for points of land in general (Louie Angalik & Mark Kalluak in Lyons 2007:36).

5.2 The House I Excavation

Description and Location

House I is a large semi-subterranean ovate structure measuring 8 x 4m in area, and 55 cm deep (see Figure 12 & 15). The perimeter is marked by a gravel berm that rises 25cm above the surface, with a 1m wide entrance passage in the middle of the western wall. These dimensions make House I remarkably different than any of the other features that are at *Ihatik* - or indeed of any other site in the vicinity of Arviat. Most Caribou Inuit dwellings at coastal sites consist of simple tent rings, 4 to 5m in diameter, which are notorious for their lack of artifacts and faunal materials within the structure (Figure 14) (see Birket-Smith 1929a: 86; Dawson 2005). An early interpretation of House I, which made it a feature of interest, was that the architecture is suggestive of a greater degree of sedentism than that of typical Caribou Inuit house features. This hypothesis was immediately supported by the large quantity of cultural materials that were found within the house during its excavation.

House I is located apart from the other features at *Ihatik*, on the very corner of the highest terrace at the easternmost edge of the site, 20m above the tidal flats of Hudson Bay (see Figure 11 & 13). Being the highest point at *Ihatik*, House I has a remarkable view of the surrounding area. To the West, the interior plain of

Figure 14 Caribou Inuit Summer Tent

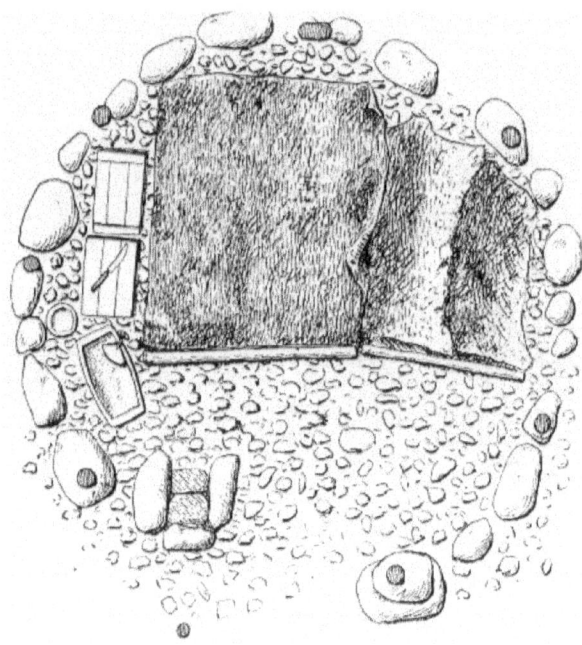

from Birket-Smith 1929a: 86

Figure 15 House I Spatial Layout and Excavation Units

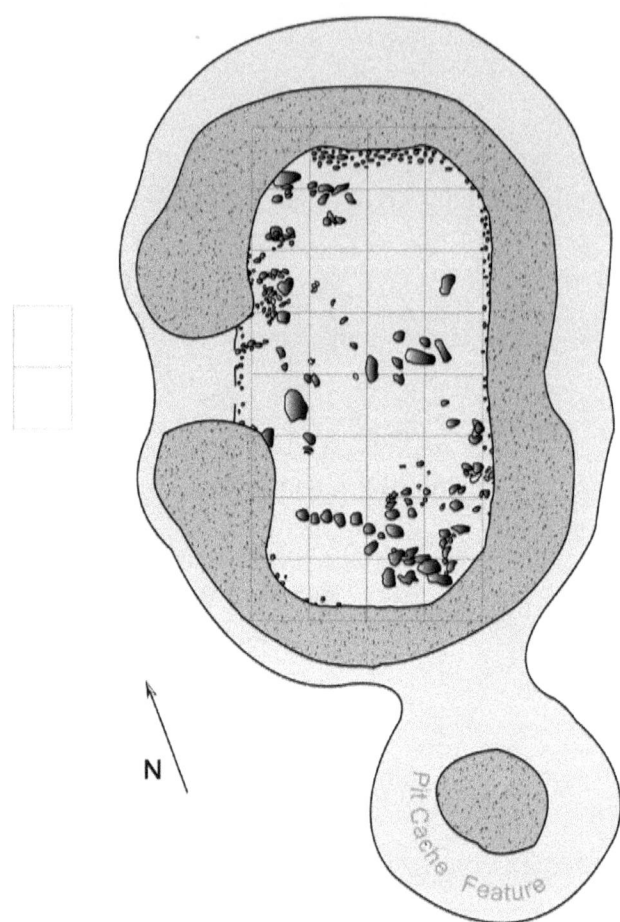

Austin Island can be seen, along with any herds of caribou that pass through the area. To the South, there are several land marks of cultural importance that can be seen including the Hamlet of Arviat, *Qikiktarrjuk*, Sentry Island (*Arviaq*), Maguse Esker, and the southern estuary of the Maguse River. To the East is Hudson Bay where seals, whales, kayaks, whale boats, and trade ships could be observed as they passed by. The North is the only blind-spot due to the configuration of the coastline. In terms of view, House I is well placed to keep close observation of the surrounding area, and vice-versa as House I is fairly conspicuous.

Methodology

House I was excavated over a two week period in July of 2006 by Dr. Peter Dawson, Luke Suluk, John Blyth, Louis Irkok, and myself. The entire house was excavated, which included thirty-two 1 x 1 metre units within the structure itself (see Figure 12 & 15). Because there was evidence of associated activity areas on the exterior of the house, two 1x1 metre units were placed in front of the entrance passage, several test pits were dug around the perimeter, collections were taken of surface deposits, and all associated cultural features were mapped and photographed. Units were initially excavated in 10 cm arbitrary levels followed by natural levels once several profiles of the stratigraphy were visible. Each unit was excavated leaving a 5 cm bulk along the unit's perimeter so that the stratigraphy of the house could be viewed in entirety once the structure was completely excavated (see Figure 12). Artifacts were recorded with three dimensions of provenience as they were found, and all fill was screened with a 1/4" mesh.

All artifacts, faunal materials, and data were transported to the University of Calgary, where they were analyzed by myself. This report divides the analysis of the House I excavation into five sections: Stratigraphy, Artifacts, Faunal Materials, Architecture, and Activity Areas.

5.3 PART 1: Stratigraphy

Excavation revealed four distinct layers in House I (see Figure 16a-c). Layer 1 was a lichen and sod mat that was consistently 7 to 8 cm in depth below the surface. Layer 2 was a dark sandy soil which contained all of the cultural material recovered during the excavation. The depth of Layer 2 varied across the house but averaged at 10-12 cm below the surface. Layer two was encountered in all units, but did not extend more than halfway up the walls of the house. Layer 3 was a thin band of dark soil that was discontinuous and free of cultural material. Layer 4 consisted of sandy gravel and represents the bottom of the house and the beginning of the geological deposit of glacial till. On average, each unit was dug to a depth of 22-25 cm below surface, or as the natural layers dictated in the case of units that included the walls of the house.

Chapter 5 – Archaeology of House I

Figure 16a Stratagraphic Profile, Facing North – House I

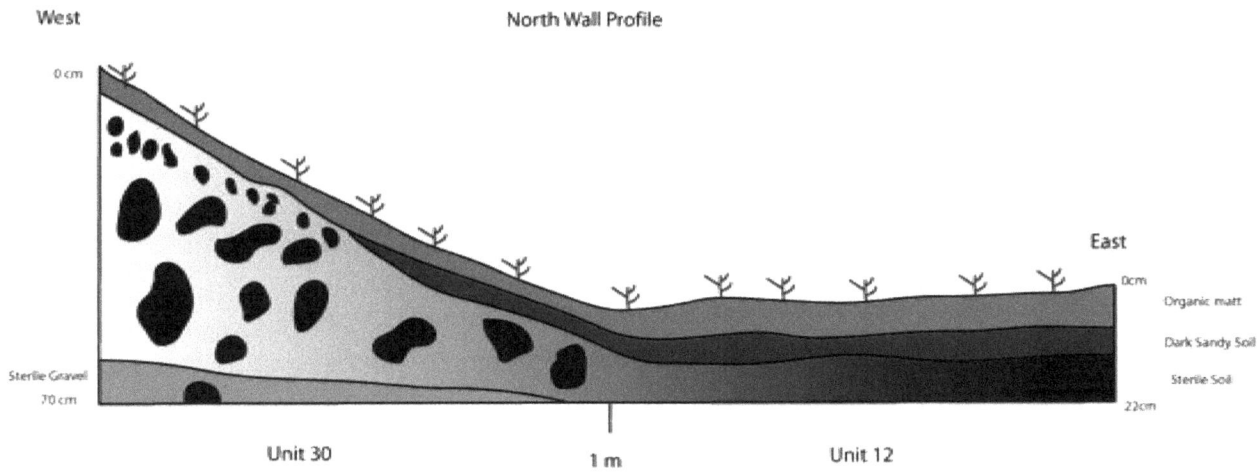

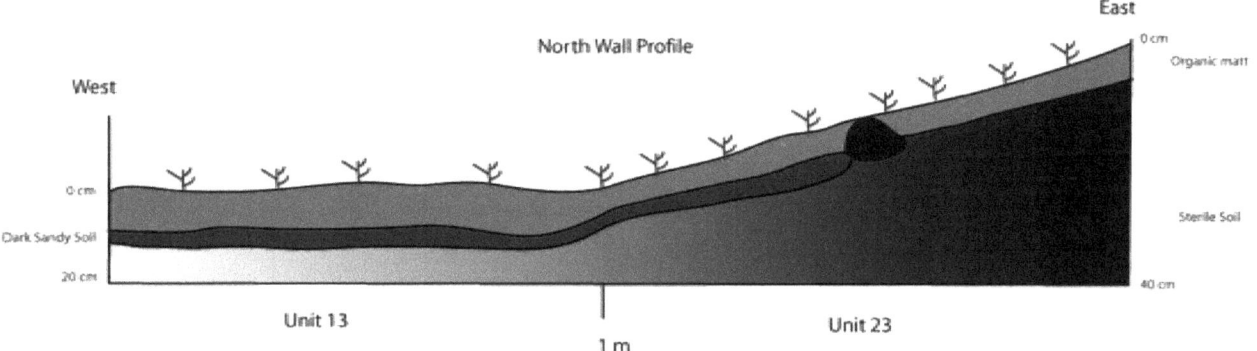

Figure 16b Stratagraphic Profile, Facing West, South Half – House I

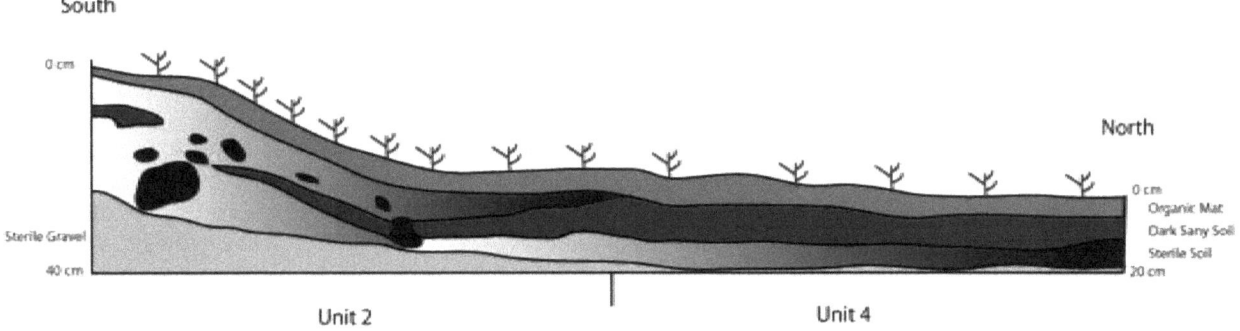

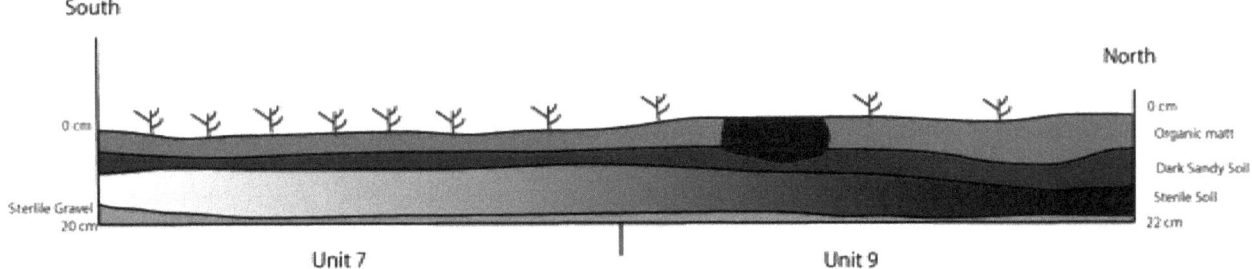

Figure 16c Stratagraphic Profile, Facing West, North Half – House I
West Wall Profile

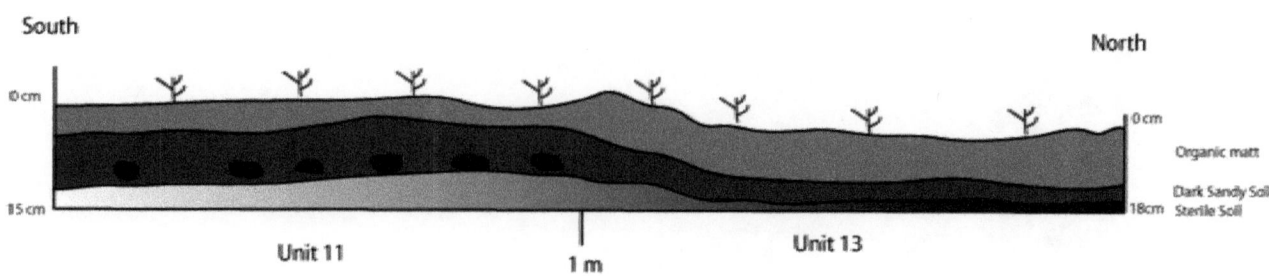

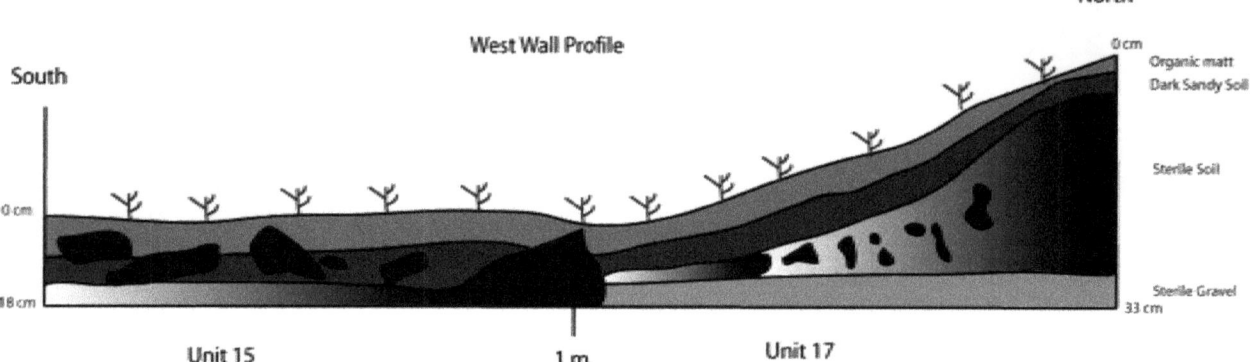

Figure 17 North Wall Composition

Preliminary Architectural Considerations

The profiled cross sections of House I show that its construction was fairly simple (see Figure 16a-c). It would seem that in building, the interior of the house was excavated to a depth of around 50 cm. The debris from the resulting depression including sod, dirt, and gravel were arranged into the ovate perimeter or 'walls' of the house; this can be seen in the profile of units that cut into those walls, as they are composed of a haphazard mixture of those materials (see Figure 17). In the middle of the western wall, a 1 m opening was left in order to form an entrance passage (see Figure 12 & 15). At the southeast corner of the house, an additional semi-subterranean chamber was built using the same techniques, with the exception that it is circular. Unfortunately, no evidence was recovered to give a definite indication of the superstructure which would have covered the house depression; no post holes were identified, and there were no sod blocks, large stones, or timbers in the fill.

5.3 PART 2: Artifacts

There are 76 artifacts in the House I assemblage which includes items of both European and Inuit manufacture. In general, preservation conditions seem to have been very good. Most of the organic artifacts are in good shape, but all of the metallic artifacts are highly corroded even though positive identification was possible in most cases.

House I Historical Artifact Descriptions

Nails

The House I assemblage contains 29 nail fragments (see Figure 19). These fragments represent a minimum number of 21 complete nails based on the presence of a head. Three basic types were recovered: hand-forged, machine-cut and wire nails, all types occurred exclusively in ferrous metals. At least 3 of the nails from House I were used for purposes other than nailing. In unit 30, which was excavated in front of the entrance passage, 3 nails were found to have been pounded into the ground in a roughly circular shape (see Figure 18). It is likely that they were used as pegs to

Chapter 5 – Archaeology of House I

Figure 18 House I Artifacts and Faunal Materials

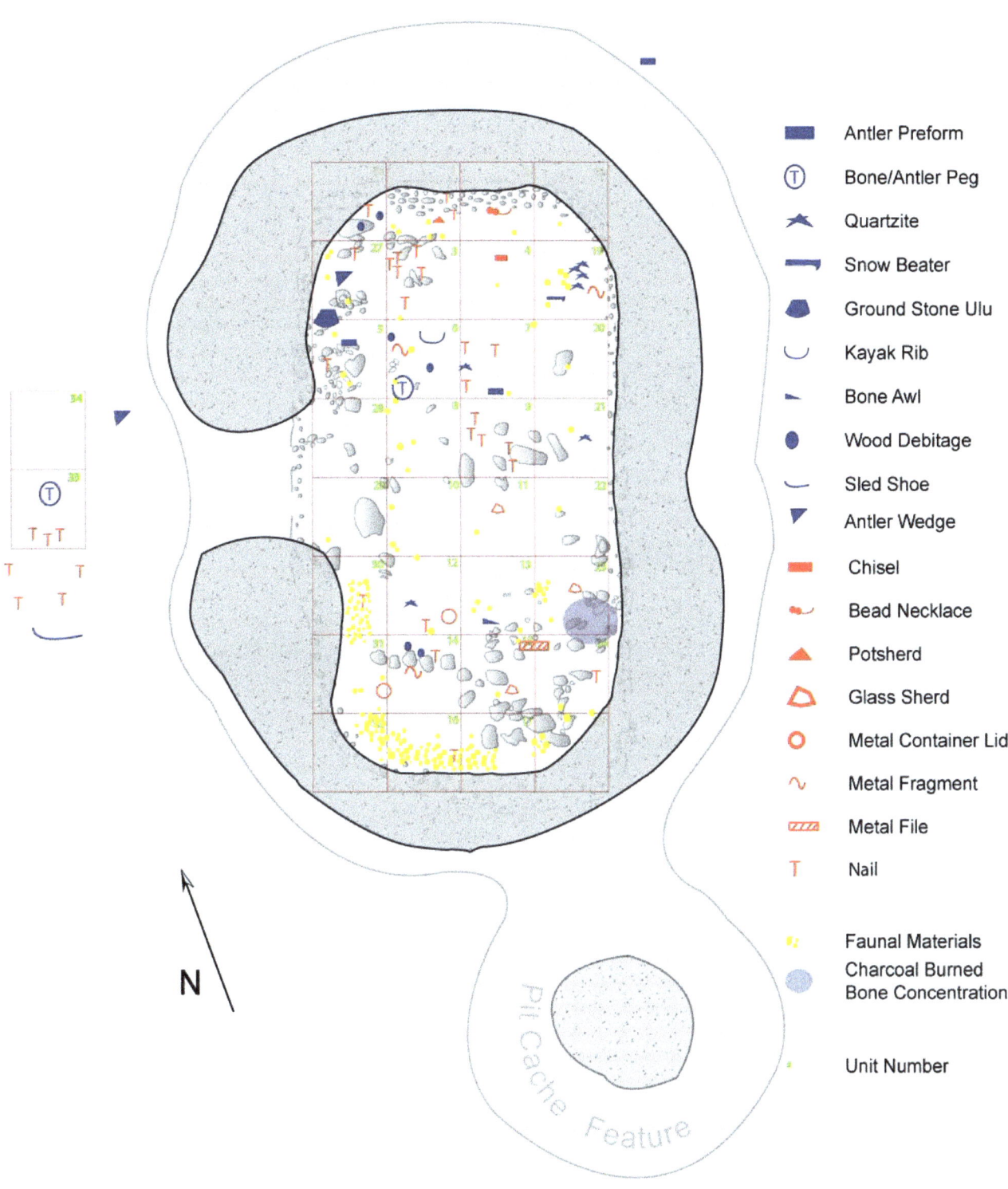

Figure 19 Nails Recovered from House I

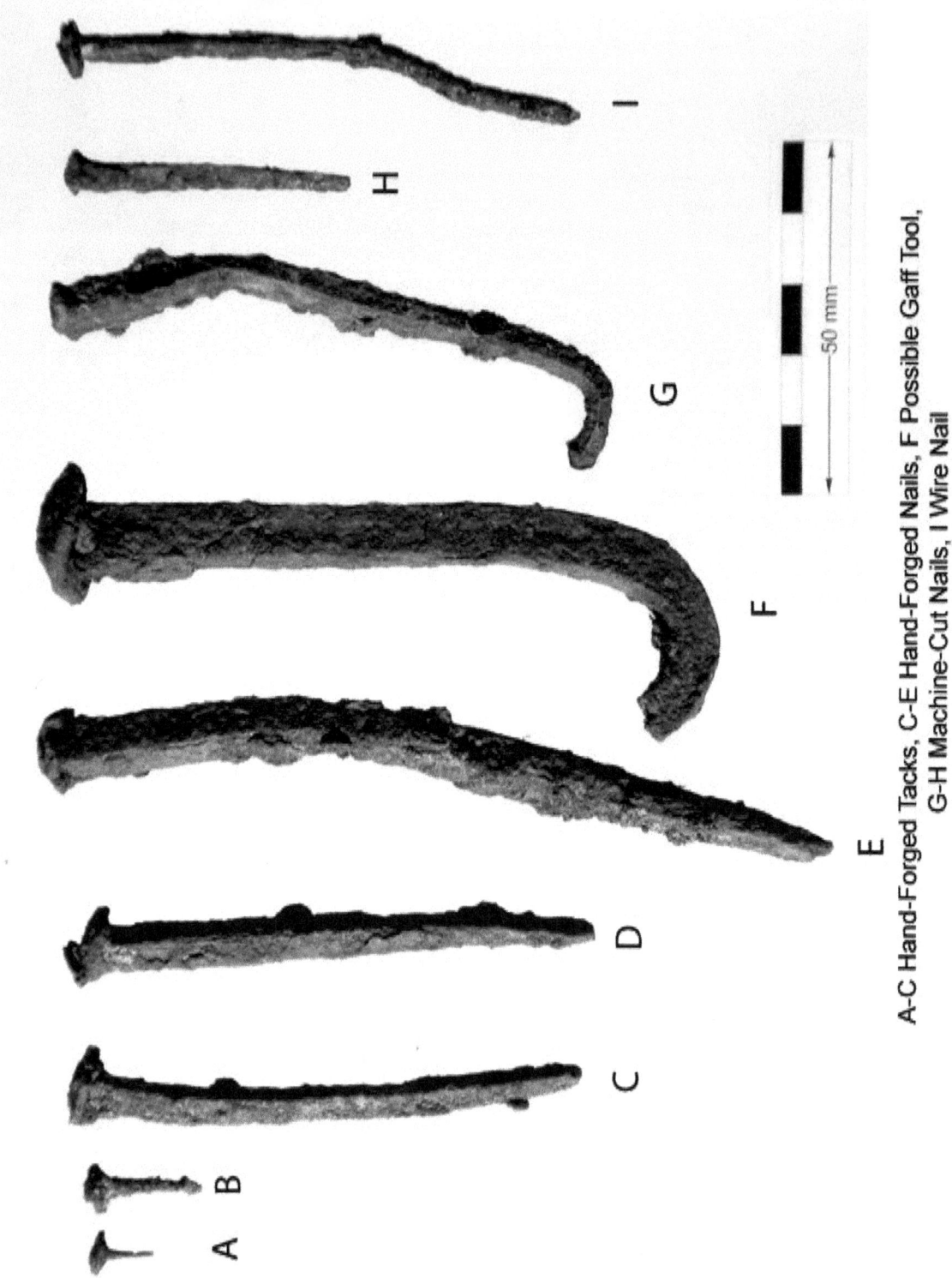

A-C Hand-Forged Tacks, C-E Hand-Forged Nails, F Possible Gaff Tool, G-H Machine-Cut Nails, I Wire Nail

stretch out skins for hide working, and were found in association with a bone peg, which supports that conclusion. As well, it is possible that some of the nails were used as parts of composite tools. One of the larger hand-forged nails appears to have been deliberately bent towards the end, possibly to form the hook for a gaff tool (see Figure 19, F).

Hand-Forged Nails (n=17): Seventeen of the nails in the House I assemblage were hand-forged. This variety can be distinguished by tapering on all sides, a lack of conformity in the shanks and heads, and a square cross section (Stone 1974:231, Wells 1998:81). Sixteen of the hand-forged nails have 'rose' heads, and only one has a flat head. Fourteen of the hand-forged nails were complete from head to tip, and 3 were broken off along the shank. There were three different size classes for the hand-forged nails: 2 tacks (<2 cm), 11 nails (<10 cm), and 4 spikes (>10 cm) (see Figure 19). Hand-forged nails were the only nails available until the invention of machine-cut nails in 1790 (Hume 1969:252; Nelson 1963:2; Wells 1998:3). However, hand-forged nails were also available well into the nineteenth century, and were used alongside machine-cut nails (Nelson 1963). Most of the hand-forged nails were likely manufactured by the blacksmiths employed at Fort Prince of Wales (see Williams & Glover 1969:243, 314). Indeed, the nails recovered from House I are stylistically similar to nails recovered by archaeologists from other HBC sites of the period (Kenyon 1985:109; Stone 1974: 236).

Machine-Cut (n=2): Machine-cut nails are differentiated from hand-forged nail based on a tapering shaft along cut faces, but a uniform thickness of the opposing sides. They were first introduced in 1790, and were made from strips of plate metal that were machine-cut to shape. In the earliest types, the heads of the machine-cut nails were hand-forged into 'rose' heads. This changed by ca. 1815 when machined heads were introduced in a variety of forms (Hume 1969:252; Nelson 1963). Only two of the nails in the House I assemblage were machine-cut (see Figure 19, G-H). One, which measured 8.2 cm, had a double-clasp head and is severely bent in two locations. The other, which measured 4.3 cm has a 'rose head'. The direction of the metal fibre is usually another diagnostic element with chronological relevance; however, both nails were too corroded for this to be determined.

Wire Nails (n=2): Wire nails were introduced to North America by the 1850s, but didn't become widely distributed until after 1875 (Hume 1969:254). They are easily distinguished from machine-cut and hand-forged nails based on the roundness and consistency of the shaft. The heads are usually 't-shaped' in cross section. There are two wire nails in the House I assemblage, both of which measure 7.6 cm in length and 0.3 cm in thickness (see Figure 19, I).

Unidentified Nail Fragments (n=8): Another 8 iron fragments that are likely pieces of nail shafts are included in the assemblage. All of them are very badly corroded, and do not have enough diagnostic features to distinguish between machine-cut and hand-forged varieties, although none of them have round cross sections.

Nails and Trade on Hudson Bay

Nails never seem to have been listed as items that were directly traded by the HBC at Churchill, nor are they listed as items requisitioned by the post during annual supply (see Williams & Glover 1969:272-280, 301-308). The post employed a Blacksmith right until the 1920s, and they would have produced all of the nails used at Churchill on-site until the point that it was more economical to import machine-cut or wire nails. If nails were items directly traded with the Inuit, they do not seem to have been listed as such. However, there is evidence that nails were sought by Inuit for use as shot as early as 1787; disused buildings around Churchill were frequently pilfered for nails and other scraps of iron that could be used as shot (Fossett 2001:119). Nails would have also been traded with the Inuit indirectly. For example, in 1821, a group of seal hunters at Seal River purchased an 'old' whaleboat (B.42/a/145). The whaleboat would certainly have contained scores of hand-forged nails and possibly machine-cut ones as well. The boat itself could have been used for decades after its purchase and would likely have been stripped of all iron once it was no longer useful. As a result, the House I assemblage could represent a normal assemblage of nails anytime after the 1850s when wire nails were first distributed, despite the high proportion of hand-forged nails.

Spatial Distribution of Nails

No definite pattern is apparent in the locations of nails found within House I, with the exception of the aforementioned 'hide pegs'. The sheer quantity of nails is interesting, and it was originally thought that the nails may have been a part of an over-arching structure that sheltered the house depression. The nails tended to be found clustered together in areas that are not likely to be representative of architectural features (see Figure 18). This indicates that rather than architectural purposes, it is more likely that the nails are associated with activities that occurred while the house was occupied.

Metal File (n=1): Metal files were among the earliest trade goods introduced to the Inuit through the HBC (Fossett 2001:93). In 1768 Andrew Graham, the Postmaster of Churchill, listed flat files as being standard items of trade and were valued at 1 Beaver, which was the unit of trade at the time (Williams & Glover 1969:273).

A single file was recovered from House I and is only 5.7 cm in length, and appears to be broken on one end (see Figure 18) (see Figure 20, A). It is a machine-made, single-cut file of the flat-bastard variety (Ross & Light 2000:23-29). Such files were designed for use on either metals or wood, but were known to have been used in practice for other ad-hoc tasks such as striking a flint. The piece is heavily corroded to the point that there is no possibility of examining the use wear.

Chisel (n=1): The assemblage contains a bit from a wood-working chisel. Chisels were also among the first items traded by the Hudson's Bay Company (Fossett 2001:95-99). Andrew Graham did not specifically mention wood-working chisels in his list of standard Hudson's Bay Company goods, but it can be assumed that one would cost approximately the same as an ice chisel which were listed as 1 beaver pelt in value (Williams & Glover 1969:273).

The wood chisel is 5.7 cm in length, with a blade that flared from 0.3 cm at the stem to 0.4 cm at the tip (see Figure 18) (see Figure 20, C). The chisel was bent in the middle, likely from use rather than design. It had a tapered neck so that it could be set into a bone or wooden handle. The tip appears to have been broken and then re-sharpened from both sides of the blade indicating that the chisel received at least some use. It is a very similar form

Caribou Inuit Traders of the Kivalliq

Figure 20 Metal Artifacts from House I

A Metal File, B Match-Box Lid (a rubbing reads "Vestas"), C Wood Chisel, D Fragment of Slip-Lid Container

to wood chisels found by archaeologists in Hudson's Bay Company posts such as Fort Michilimackinac and Fort Albany (Stone 1974:302).

Bead & Copper Ornament: (n=1): A bead and copper ornament was recovered that was likely a part of a necklace (see Figure 18) (see Figure 21, B). It consisted of two white wire-drawn glass beads that were tied together with a piece of sinew. Neither of the beads was larger

Chapter 5 – Archaeology of House I

Figure 21 Ground-Slate Ulu and Bead/Copper Ornament from House I

A Ground-Slate Ulu (Women's Knive), B Bead and Copper Ornament (note sinew string holding the glass beads together)

than 0.2 cm and both were encased in a copper tube that was conical in shape. Beads were one of the most popular trade goods, and Andrew Graham reports that in 1766 alone, Churchill Post requisitioned 13 lbs of small white glass beads (Williams & Glover 1969:302). Although there were many different colour patterns and sizes, small plain-white beads are a common find in Hudson's Bay Company posts (Stone 1974:94-112). Beads were highly sought after by Caribou Inuit, and were used to decorate men and women's clothing, hide bags, and needle cushions (Karklins 1992:208)

Slide-box Runner (n=1): One piece of wood that was recovered from the site was obviously a hard wood, and had been crafted using precise carpentry tools. It consisted of a toothed groove that may have been the runner for a slide-open box such as that which a telescope or binoculars might be carried in.

Container Lid (n=1): Slip-lid containers were used in North America from the mid 1700s onwards, but only became widely popular after the 1850s and were usually used for dry goods such as tea, snuff, and tobacco (Davis 1967: 71-76). The containers consisted of a lipped mouth over which a tightly matched lid was fitted. Two iron fragments of a slip-lid container were recovered (see Figure 18) (see Figure 20, D). Both fragments were in poor shape, so little can be deduced about the size and shape of the containers that they came from, but both are fragments of the lid (see Paine 1977).

Clear Glass (n=2): The assemblage contains two pieces of transparent glass. Both are 0.2 cm thick and came from a cylindrical container (see Figure 18). Both pieces were so small that no other diagnostic features could be determined.

Pale Blue Glass (n=1): A single piece of pale blue glass was recovered (see Figure 18). It came from a container that had a spherical exterior in at least one place. Although techniques to colour glass predate Columbus, Jones (2000:147) points out that it became very fashionable in the 1880s for all types of glass wares from the cheapest to the most expensive to be coloured, and specifically mentions pale blue as being a popular choice.

Ceramic (n=1): There is only one ceramic artifact in the House I assemblage. It is a rim shard from an earthenware jar that had an 8 cm diameter mouth (see Figure 18). The piece has a moderate out flare in cross section, and is lipped on the outside of the pot. The temper is fine and a light brown colour. The shard is polychrome, with light brown on the exterior, a green band around the inside lip, and a white on the interior. The shard is also glazed.

Match-box Lid (n=1): A single brass lid cover for a match box was identified (see Figure 20, B). The lid is 7.2 cm in length, 3.7 cm in width and weighs 9.1 grams. There is a small bar that runs the length of one side and would have formed a simple hinge with the bottom of the container. Although heavily corroded, the lid clearly has a stamp which reads "Vestas".

Iron Fragments (n=2): There were two iron fragments that were in too corroded a condition to be properly identified. One was 6.7 cm in length and the other 3.2 cm.

Sheet Metal (n=2): Two pieces sheet tin (0.02 cm thickness) were recovered. They were likely part of some sort of packaging.

Copper Fragments (n=1): A single unidentifiable copper strip, 6.1 mm long, and decorated with a groove down the middle was recovered from the site. It was likely an element of packaging of some kind, perhaps the seal from a bottle.

House I Bone, Antler, and Stone Artifact Descriptions

Antler Wedge (n=1): An antler wedge was found to the north of the entrance passage of House I (see Figure 18) (see Figure 22, A). It consists of half an antler shaft that appears to have been separated by the split-and-wedge technique as demonstrated by the slight inwards curve along all of the edges of the piece where a groove would have been scored using a burin. However, the piece also has several surfaces that were clearly sawn as the tooth marks from the saw are still visible. There are also a couple of deep marks which would have likely been made by a metal knife blade. The wedge is quite large at 15.1 cm in length and 4.6 cm in width. The tip of the wedge is very narrow and has been polished through use. The reverse end of the antler has a platform that has multiple marks where it was pounded.

Antler Wedge Preform (n=1): A piece of antler measuring 6.1 cm in length and 4.7 cm in width and having several characteristics of a wedge was recovered in unit 5 (see Figure 18). The object has been deliberately bevelled into a wedge shape on one side, but is too poorly preserved to determine if it had been used as such. The striking surface of the wedge consists of a clean saw line that does not display any signs of pounding. The object could certainly have been used as a wedge, but would likely have had several finishing features added before use. For example, the wedge tapers dramatically from the tip to the striking surface. This likely would have been levelled off if it were to be used as a wedge.

Bird Dart/Fishing Leister Preform (n=1): An object that is likely a preform for a barbed point was collected from the surface of the site to the northeast of the house (see Figure 18) (see Figure 22, E). It is a Beluga whale scapula fragment (11.1 cm x 7.3 cm) that is carved into two barbs along the posterior edge. It appears to have only been half-made before discard. The next step would have been to sharpen the barbs and then score a line down the scapula to remove the barbed point. The completed point would likely have been used on either a fishing leister, or a prong on a bird dart.

Kayak Rib (n=1): One piece of wood recovered is likely a fragment from a kayak rib. It is 4.4 cm in length and weighs 2.5 grams (see Figure 18). The piece has been deliberately carved so that it is sharpened towards one end. In his documentation of Caribou Inuit kayak construction, Arima (1975:120) points out that this was done in order that the ribs could be inserted into holes drilled in the gunwale planks. The piece of wood has also been carved along the grain of the wood perfectly, and is curved slightly which may indicate that the rib was broken during the bending process. It is also bevelled along the inside edge of the curve in order to assist with the bending process. The piece of wood is also charred on one side indicating that it was exposed to fire.

Antler Peg (n=1): A single antler peg was excavated in unit six. It measures 7.1 cm and has been sawn off at the burr end of the antler (see Figure 15) (See Figure 22, B). The tip is poorly preserved, but appears to have been worked into a point.

Bone Peg (n=1): A seal tibia in unit 33 was excavated in an upright position as though it had been pounded into the ground (see Figure 18) (see Figure 22, C). The tip is worn from use and it was found in association with the ring of iron nails that had also been pounded upright into the ground.

Figure 22 Antler and Bone Tools from House I

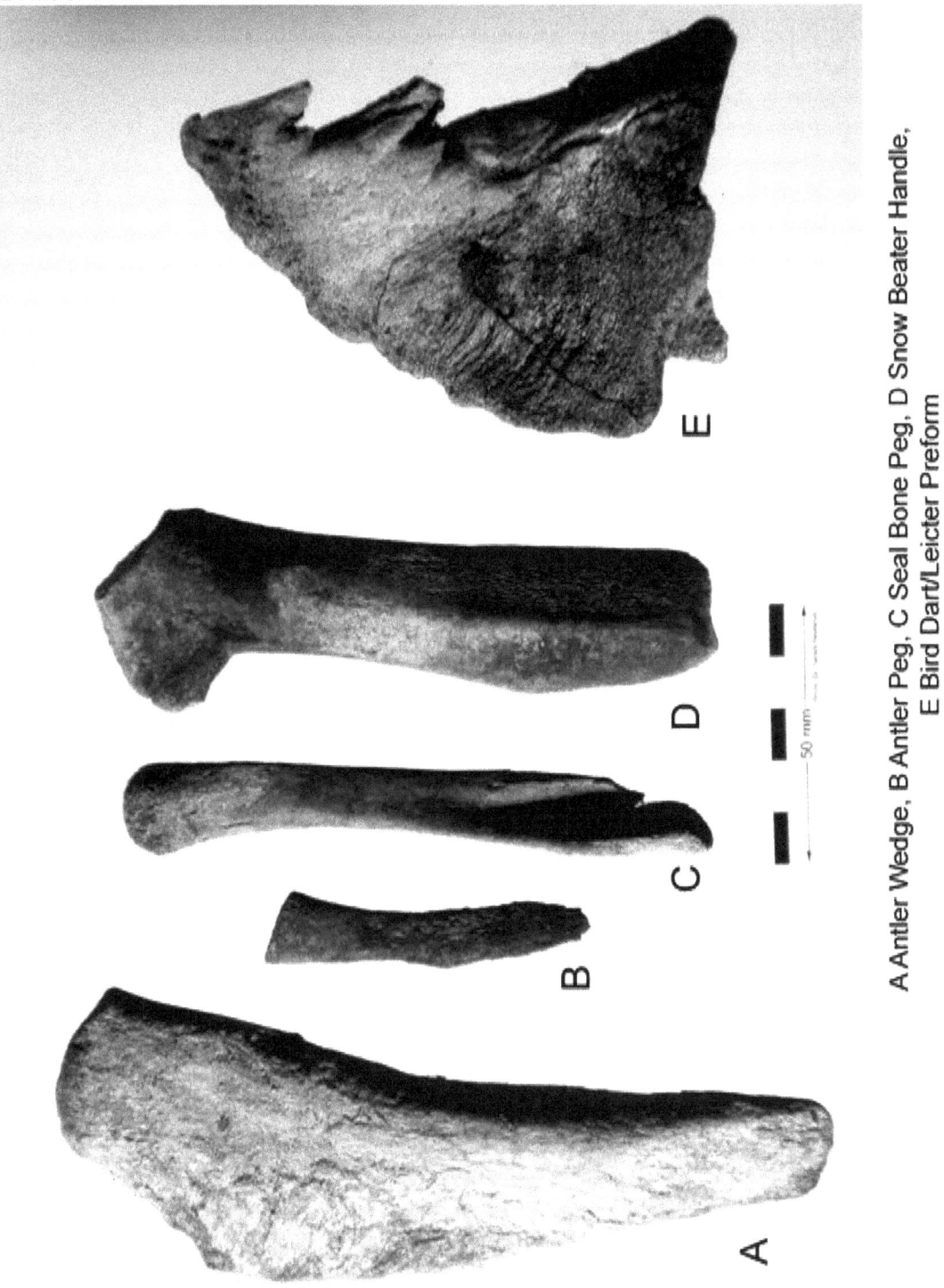

A Antler Wedge, B Antler Peg, C Seal Bone Peg, D Snow Beater Handle, E Bird Dart/Leicter Preform

Bone Awl (n=1): A small bone awl, 4.4cm in length, was recovered in unit 13 (see Figure 18). The piece has a bevelled tip that has polish on it from use. At the top of the tool, there are several gouge marks that indicate that someone may have attempted to turn the tool into a needle at some time. The shaft is probably too wide though, and would have had to be modified further for use as a needle. Given the small nature of the tool, it would have almost certainly been hafted into a handle of some sort. The bone element from which the bone awl was made could not be identified.

Snow Beater Handle (n=1): A common tool found in Inuit households across the arctic is the snow beater. It is used to brush snow off of clothing before entering the house. A bone tool measuring 12.7 cm was found in unit #19 and closely resembles the handles of the snow beaters that Birket-Smith described for the area (see Figure 18) (see Figure 22, B) (Birket-Smith 1929:305). The piece has several locations that have either saw-marks, or cut marks. It also has a surface that has been bevelled, and other parts of the tool are polished smooth

Caribou Inuit Traders of the Kivalliq

either as a part of its construction or use. The piece has been broken off at the end, so there is no way to tell if it would have extended into an adjoined blade, or if it would have been hafted to a blade as a separate piece. There are no drill holes at the end which would have indicated that this was a snow knife handle rather than a snow beater.

Sled Shoe (n=1): An antler object with two wrought iron nails in it was collected from the surface next to House I (see Figure 18). It appears to be a runner for a sled and is very similar in shape and size (17.4 cm) to a whale-bone sled shoe recovered from Nuvuq Point (JgKm-1) in 2003 (Dawson 2005:47). Caribou Inuit sleds were constructed using wood and could be up to 10 meters in length. Birket-Smith (1929:176) observed that the longer traveling sledges were never fitted with permanent shoes when snow conditions were good. However, as warm spring weather began to melt the peat-layer used to cover the runner, sled shoes of whale bone and walrus ivory were substituted to decrease friction.

Ground Stone Ulu (n=1): Birket-Smith (1929:140) describes ulu blades as "the women's knives" - a pattern of association recognized across the Arctic. Ulus were used by women to cut meat, and also scrape hides. A ground slate ulu was found close to the West wall, just North of the entrance passage (see Figure 18) (see Figure 21, A). It is made of a dark slate that has several bedding planes within the material. The blade is 5.7 cm long and the neck 2.9 cm at its narrowest. The whole piece was 6.4 cm long. The blade had recently been sharpened, but does display some use-wear along the cutting endge of the blade. The neck of the ulu itself has been chipped in a number of locations for hafting purposes.

Lithic Debitage

There are 8 pieces of lithic debitage in the House I assemblage weighing a total of 105.9g (see Figure 18). All were of the same material, a white/yellow coarse grained quartzite which was the same material as found on Nuvuq Point (Dawson 2005:49-51).

Core (n=1): One piece was a small core that measured 3.4 cm in length. It had 5 flake scars on it with some evidence of platform grinding on one surface. Half of the core is covered in cortex which suggests that it was part of a small cobble to begin with.

Utilized Flakes (n=1): One large flake (6.9 cm) appeared to have use wear on one of its edges.

Flakes (n=3): Three small flakes were recovered, all with well defined platforms and ventral surfaces. Two of them measured 2.9 cm, while the third was 1.5 cm. All seem to be shaping or tertiary flakes associated with the final stages of reduction.

Shatter (n=1): One piece of shatter 2.6 cm in length was recovered.

Gunflints (n=2): One small lithic piece measuring 2.6 cm in length has deliberate modification around the tip creating an angle that would normally be associated with a scraping tool, but the modification is not smooth or consistent. It resembles in shape a gun flint and may in fact be one even though its form is very rough. There was no obvious use wear, and the modification could possibly be from firing strikes. It would certainly be the correct size and shape to fit comfortably into the vice of a flint-lock rifle. Another piece was a small bifacially worked wedge-shape which would also have fit nicely into a flint-lock.

Charcoal (n=58): 58 fragments of burned wood were recovered from House I. Most of them are associated with the hearth feature located in unit 15. The majority of the burned pieces appeared to be small twigs such as willow, however some were clearly from larger pieces of softwood that were either driftwood or trade wood.

Wood (n=5): Several pieces of wood that displayed obvious signs of having been worked with metal trade tools are also indicative of construction activities within the house (see Figure 18). This included a piece that was sawn on one end, and had a surface that was sanded, and then painted. Another piece had several drilled holes, and a groove carved down the middle. As well, there was a fragment of a wooden shaft 8cm long and 0.6 cm wide that had been deliberately carved along the grain of the wood, and was broken on both ends. Although the function of any these pieces probably does not exceed that of debris, it likely demonstrates that wood working was an activity that occurred within the house.

House I Artifacts Chronology

When the chronology of European trade on Hudson Bay is considered together with the assortment of historical artifacts recovered from House I, it can be seen that the assemblage was most likely deposited in the late 1800s. The presence of wire nails, slip-lid containers and pale blue glass, places the 1850s as the absolute earliest date or *terminus post quem* (TPQ) of the assemblage based on invention and distribution of those products. It is more difficult to place an upper chronological limit on the assemblage, but there are a suite of products introduced around 1900 that were absent in House I. Most notably, this includes ammunition cartridges, which rapidly replaced muskets in HBC trade between the 1880s and 1900 (see Piers 1934:63; Fossett 2001:176-177). As well, there are a number of tin containers such as key-lid and open-top cans which became widely used around the same time which are also absent in the assemblage. Throughout the *Ihatik* site, cartridges for Lee-Enfield and Martini Henry rifles, along with key-lid and open-top cans, are densely scattered in surface middens, tent-rings, graves and just about any other archaeological feature (Dawson et al. 2007). The complete absence of these products in the House I assemblage is strong evidence that the assemblage was probably deposited before 1900 A.D.

Table 8 House I Artifact Quantities and Representation

Artifact	Quantity	Percent of Total Assemblage	Category
European Artifacts		65 %	
Nails (including fragments)	29		Construction
Chisel	1		Construction
Bead and Copper Ornament	1		Decorative
Container Lid	1		Household
Clear Glass	2		Household
Pale Blue Glass	1		Household
Ceramic	1		Household
Matchbox Lid	1		Household
Iron Fragments	2		Construction
Sheet Metal	2		Construction
Copper Fragment	1		Construction
Inuit Artifacts		35%	
Antler Wedge	1		Construction
Antler Wedge Preform	1		Construction
Bird Dart Preform	1		Construction
Kayak Rib	1		Construction
Antler Peg	1		Household
Bone Peg	1		Household
Bone Awl	1		Household
Snow Beater Handle	1		Household
Sled Shoe	1		Transportation
Ground Stone Ulu	1		Food Preparation
Lithics	8		Construction
Charcoal	58	* Not included	Food Preparation
Wood Fragments	5	* Not included	Construction

Traditional and European Artifacts

The artifact assemblage, although containing European items, is distinctly representative of an Inuit household. This is most obviously illustrated by the traditional items that are made of local materials including the ulu, snow-beater, bone awl, bone and antler pegs, lithics for striking fire, etc. In spite of the strangeness in architecture, such artifacts represent activities that normally occur in Caribou Inuit dwellings; construction, household tasks, and food preparation (see Table 8) (see Birket-Smith 1929a). Construction seems to have been a major activity that occurred in the house as evidenced by the large number of tools, wood debitage, and half-formed tools. The construction assemblage is also distinctly Inuit in the use of wedges, as well as the items that were actually being formed such as the bird dart, and the kayak rib. Furthermore, the European items that are in the assemblage are representative of items that were traded TO the Inuit: containers, beads, files, chisels, etc.

There is an interesting pattern in the ways which Inuit and European items combine to form the assemblage. In bulk percentage, European items account for 65% of the artifacts (see Table 8). However, it is important to note that without exception, none of the European artifacts in the assemblage replace traditional technologies, but rather supplement them. Some of the most popular HBC trade goods included wood working tools such as knives, saws, and files etc., and indeed construction seems to have been a major activity in and around House I (see Figure 18). The presence of two wedges is particularly interesting. Wedges are used in the 'split and wedge' technique, a traditional method to reduce pieces of wood lengthways along the grain, and are a common element of hunter-gatherer tool kits around the world as no metallic implements are required (Adney & Chapelle 194:18-19). This work can technically be replaced by the rip saw, which is the technique that European carpenters would use. Even though a saw was not recovered, there are saw marks on many of the tools, preforms, and debitage indicating that the occupants of the house did indeed own one. Ironically enough, the wedges themselves were actually crafted using a saw, yet the wedge technique seems to have still been a construction practice. The ultimate products of construction, such as fishing leisters and kayaks, are not different than what would have been built using a strictly traditional tool kit either. The nails and containers are also indicative of activities that could have been performed without European goods.

5.3 PART 3: House I Faunal Analysis

The House I faunal assemblage, with 2498 specimens, is the largest that has ever been recovered from a single structure in the Arviat region. The scale of recovery may reflect a greater permanency in residence than other Caribou Inuit structures found in the region, but excellent preservation conditions are certainly a factor as well. All specimens were collected during the complete excavation of House I in the summer of 2006. The provenience of each specimen was recorded by the unit in which it was found. The assemblage also includes the faunal materials that were retained by the ¼" mesh through which all dirt was screened. The specimens were then transported to the University of Calgary, where I analyzed the complete assemblage using the Archaeology Department's comparative collection.

A. Observational, Ethnographic and Ecological Data

Preservation of bone in House I was excellent; 1898 out of 2498 specimens, or 76% of the assemblage, were positively identified as a result. In the Appendix, Table 9 displays a summary of the identifications including the number of identified specimens (NISP), the minimum number of individuals (MNI), and the most common element (MCE) used to create the MNI. An elaboration of the bones that were used in calculating the MNI is available. MNI was simply calculated as the most common element from each species (see Table 9).

Nature of the Assemblage

Human activity, generally relating to hunting and butchery, often leaves patterns of bone which, if preserved, can be excavated and studied by archaeologists. The specimens recovered from House I must be treated as a sample assemblage of the deposited assemblage (see Ringrose 1993:123-124). Before any zooarchaeological interpretations can be made, the relationship between these two assemblages must be assessed by examining a number of taphonomic processes that could have modified the faunal remains since their deposition. Although there have been numerous attempts to predict and quantify fossil histories of assemblages by estimating the magnitude of taphonomic processes (see Hedges & Millard 1995a; Hedges & Millard 1995b; Lyman 1984; Lyman 1985; Ringrose 1993:139; Rogers 2000), this report favours a simplified approach that relies primarily on qualitative observations to assess the amount of confidence that can be placed in the House I sample assemblage.

Diagenesis - the chemical, physical, and microbial degradation of bone - does not seem to have been a major taphonomic process at work on the House I faunal assemblage. Several bones were moderately weathered on one side indicating that some of the bones were exposed to the elements at some point, but the damage was not at a level that hindered the identification process. Fish bone is a good indicator fossil in this assessment; 962 bones of *Salvelinus alpinus* (Arctic char) were recovered including the most fragile of cranial bones such as opercles. Nicholson (1996:517, 520-522) shows that fish bone degrades more quickly than mammalian or avian bone in soils of various acidities, is more likely to suffer damage from microbial agents, and is also more susceptible to physical weathering by such agents as wind, water, ice, and sunlight. The presence of fish bone, in such quantity and condition as those from House I, is a good indication that specimen losses due to diagenetic forces are negligible.

Damage and consumption of bone by carnivores during and after archaeological deposition is a common taphonomic process, especially at Arctic sites due to the presence of domestic and wild animals that live in close association with humans (Whitridge 2001:24). This process is easily detected by the presence of gnaw marks on bones - a normal observation for most Arctic assemblages (see Leblanc 1994). Of the 2498 bones recovered from House I, I only identified 1 as having evidence of carnivore modification. While very unusual, this demonstrates that specimen losses to carnivores are also insignificant. Only 5.8% of the sample assemblage exhibited signs of human modification such as cut marks, impact marks, spiral fractures, or burning.

The recovery and analytical strategies used to produce the sample assemblage must also be scrutinized. For example, the use of ¼" screens during the excavation of House I has biased the assemblage because most faunal specimens smaller than ¼" are presumably lost. Lyman (1994:55) and Ringrose (1993) point out that the tenacity and skill of the analyst can severely impact even the most basic zooarchaeological analytical units, such as MNI. I was unable to identify only 14% of the sample assemblage; while I am confident in my results, it is acknowledged that another analyst could have made slightly different identifications and thus produced a different sample assemblage.

Overall, the sample assemblage appears to have a relatively good relationship to the deposited assemblage; there are no obvious signs to suggest otherwise. In a regional context this is significant as there are no other sites in the Arviat region that have yielded

Table 9 Summary of House I Faunal Assemblage

Taxon	NISP	MNI	MNI Criteria
AVES			
Branta (goose)	3	1	L Humerus
BIVALVIA			
Mytilidae edulis (mussels)	71	24	Beaks /2
Ostreidae pectinidae (scallops)	17	5	Beaks /2
Pelycypoda (clams)	15	6	Beaks /2
MAMMALIA			
Pinnipeds			
Pusa hispida/ Phoca vitulina (Ringed and Harbour seals)	562	10	L Scapula
Erignathus barbatus (Bearded Seal)	1	1	L Metatarsal (1st)
Rangifer tarandus (Caribou)	268	6	L Metatarsal
Lagomorpha (Arctic hare)	1	1	L Maxilla
Ursus maritimus (Polar bear)	1	1	R Temporalis
Delhpinapterus leucas (Beluga)	1	1	L Rib
PISCES			
Salvelinus alpinus (Arctic char)	959	8	L Basiptrygium
UNIDENTIFIABLE	599		
Totals	2498		

such a large faunal assemblage from within a single structure.

Species

The representation of taxa in the House I assemblage closely reflects the taxa available on Austin Island and its vicinity with a couple of notable exceptions. The eastern shore of the Island provides access to all of the marine resources in the assemblage including seals, char, beluga, and shellfish (see Figure 10). The North and South arm of the Maguse River also provide access to char, and can be crossed by the terrestrial animals that are present: caribou, and polar bear (see Figure 10). Finally, the Island has many ponds and sloughs that are excellent nesting grounds for waterfowl. Also available on Austin Island, but absent in the assemblage, are foxes, wolves, wolverines, rabbits and other rodents. Birket-Smith (1929a: 113-114) suggests that small mammals were occasionally eaten by the Caribou Inuit, but that they did not form any major part of the diet. The complete absence of bones from fur-bearing terrestrial mammals is particularly interesting in the context of the time-frame that House I was occupied, as furs were of high economic value due to HBC trade (see Chapter 4).

Pinnipedia (Seals)

A total of 563 seal bones were positively identified in the House I assemblage, representing no less than 11 individuals. This is approximately 25% of the total faunal assemblage for the house, making seals one of the dominant species recovered (see Table 9). The University of Calgary comparative collection contains several *Pinnipeds*, but none are articulated, and the exact species of all samples is not certain. While bone could be positively identified as *Phocidae*, it was more difficult to refine the diagnosis to species. *Pusa hispida* (Ringed seal), and *Phoca vitulina* (Harbour seal), both of which are present in the Austin Island waters, were indistinguishable as a result. Harp seals (*Phoca groenlandica*), do occasionally visit the area, but sightings south of Rankin Inlet are extremely rare, and they are not considered in this report as a result (see Figure 1) (Mansfield 1968:383). A single phalange of an

Caribou Inuit Traders of the Kivalliq

Erignathus barbatus (Bearded seal), was easily distinguished from Ringed and Harbour seal specimens based on larger size and unique morphology.

Seals at Ihatik

Ringed, Harbour, and Bearded seals, can all be found around Austin Island, but seasonality is a factor in distribution. In the warm season, small populations of Bearded and Harbour seals are available. Estuaries, such as those of the Maguse on the North and South end of Austin Island, are ideal grounds to hunt Harbour seals as they feed at such fresh-water outlets (Louie Angalik in Dawson et al. 2006: 68). Occasionally, Harbour seals can even be found in the rivers and lakes that drain into Hudson's Bay - as far as 200 km in the case of Ranger Seal Lake (Mansfield 1968:382-383). Bearded seals usually migrate with the pack ice, but can occasionally be found in the summer, also located in the estuaries where they haul themselves onto rocks or sand bars to rest (Mansfield 1968:381). Birket-Smith (1929a:131-132) interviewed some Padlirmiut at Arviat who recalled hunting seals from kayaks in the summer during the late 19th century. As with other Inuit, Padlirmiut hunted with toggling harpoons that were launched from throwing boards and were attached with a line to bladder floats. The harpoon was later replaced with the gun, and the kayak with the whaling boat (Arima 1975:155). Throughout the historic period, seal products were the main item of trade on the part of Inuit during the summer. An excellent example is the summer sealing camp that was maintained by the Homeguards at the estuary of Seal River during the 1800s (see Chapter 4).

Winter is also an ideal time for seal hunting at *Ihatik* (Donald Uluadluak & Louie Angalik in Dawson et al. 2006: 66-71). This is the result of the stable land-fast ice that develops along the shore in the Arviat region. This land-fast ice meets a floe-edge that is only 5-15 km off-shore depending on the year (Lunn et al. 1997: 915; Riewe 1991: 5-6). The land-fast ice begins to form in November and doesn't break up until July. The transitional zone from land-fast ice to free-moving pack ice is prime hunting ground for Ringed and Bearded seals, which have the ability to create breathing holes. Inuit across the Arctic have hunted seals through breathing holes, patiently poised with toggling harpoons until a seal surfaces for air (Balikci 1970: 67-76, Boas 1964: 68; Smith 1975: 175; Smith et al. 1991). Birket-Smith (1929a) suggests that winter sealing was not a part of the Caribou Inuit cultural pattern at the time of his ethnography, but they were in contact with groups such as the Aivilingmiut and Netsilik who did.

Rangifer tarandus (Caribou)

Of the faunal assemblage, 268 of the specimens were identified as caribou, representing no less than 6 individuals (see Table 9). Caribou are ubiquitous in the Kivalliq, but only those of the Qamanirjuaq herd can be found at the coastal regions (Riewe 1992: 191). Caribou are only available during the spring, summer, and fall. In the Spring, they travel north through the Arviat region on their way to the calving grounds at Qamanirjuaq Lake (see Figure 2). Caribou are usually weak from the winter at this time of year; their meat is lean, and their hides are of poor quality due to infestations of Warble flies (Macpherson 1968: 481-483). The Caribou return to the area later in the summer and early fall before they migrate southwards to the tree-line for the winter. Movement of the herd as it passes through the Arviat region is influenced heavily by topography. Rivers in particular are obstructions, and caribou rely on crossings where the current is less severe (Arima 1984: 448-449). There are crossings which allow the caribou to access Austin Island itself (see Figure 10).

In the winters, after the caribou migrated south, the Caribou Inuit relied on cached meat that had been prepared during the summer and fall (Burch 1986:121). Winter dwellings were carefully placed so that they would be within travelling distance of these caches, and the meat would be brought back to the house from there (Bennett & Rowley 2004:247). In order to cache the meat, it has to be processed so that it will preserve. During the warmest parts of the summer, caribou meat must be dried so that it will not rot. In this process, meat is completely separated from the bone due to the fact that marrow putrefies quickly. Strips of meat are cut and dried on racks before they are bundled in caribou skins and carefully placed in rock caches. Meat that is unable to be cached is eaten as the caribou are caught. This generally includes marrow, bone grease, organs, and lower limbs which are boiled to make a broth – a summer delicacy (Rasmussen 1930:43). As the temperature declines towards the end of September, it becomes possible to cache meat with bone whole on account of refrigeration. This is very convenient as Inuit are very busy accumulating stores for the winter at this point in time thus increasing the number of 'riders' that will accompany cached meat; however, there isn't very much ethnographic data to confirm what types of minimal preparations may take place and their effect on bones that might get preserved (Luke Suluk 2007: personal communication).

Salvelinus alpinus (Arctic Char)

Arctic char bones were the dominant species in the assemblage with 959 specimens representing no less than 8 individuals (see Table 9). Preservation of fish bone was exceptional, and in general, many elements were preserved whole with little to no fragmentation – even in the case of the more fragile cranial bones. This permitted good identifications of bone, and each specimen was rigorously checked against Arctic cod and Trout in the comparative collection. As a result, all of the fish bones were positively identified as belonging to the *Salmonidae* family, which consists only of Arctic char in Hudson's Bay (Hunter 1968:363).

Arctic char are anadromous fish that start life in lakes and rivers. In the late winter to early spring, Arctic char migrate from interior lakes, down rivers such as the

Maguse to the ocean. In the late-summer to early-fall they spawn, following the same rivers back to the lakes where they were born in order to breed (Hunter 1968: 362-363). The fall spawn is an ideal time to hunt Arctic char, and Inuit families made great preparations for the spawn in order to cache enough fish for the winter. *Saputit* (fishing weirs) were built to trap Arctic char during the spawning so that Inuit families could spear the fish using *kakivak* (fishing leisters) from the shore (Burch 1986:121). Fall fishing was usually very successful, and fish were immediately cleaned, filleted, and dried, so that they could be cached for the winter. In some years, the catch was so great that the work became too tiring for the women who generally did the processing. In this case, as many fish were dried as possible, and the rest were simply cleaned and then cached whole (Bennett & Rowley 2004: 252).

Bivalvia (Shellfish)

There were 103 specimens of shellfish that were recovered, which included 71 *Edulis mytilidae* (Mussels), 17 *Ostreidae pectinidae* (Scallops) and 15 *Pelycypoda* (Clams). There is no ethnographic data on Caribou Inuit use of shellfish, but they have shown up in other Caribou Inuit sites situated on the coast and shellfish are commonly eaten by people in the community of Arviat at present (Dawson 2005:35). All three species can be found in large quantities in the tidal flats of Hudson Bay below the *Ihatik* site, and would be available at any time of the year when the Bay was not frozen (see Figure 11).

Branta (Geese)

Three bones were identified as belonging to the *Branta* genus, which on Austin Island could include Canada geese (*Branta canadensis*), or Snow geese (*Branta caerulescens*) (Cooch 1968: 447-448). Austin Island is full of ponds and swamps which attract geese that migrate to the region in the spring to nest. Geese can nest in flocks of up to 1200 per square kilometre making them a ubiquitous resource. Geese and eggs are easy to find and harvest during this period as nests can reveal large quantities of eggs, and adults are not quick to abandon their nests or goslings once hatched. The geese begin to migrate at the beginning of September and are completely gone by the end of October (Cooch 1968).

Delphinapterus Leucas (Beluga Whale)

A single rib from a Beluga whale was recovered from House I. Belugas can be found in the estuaries of the Maguse River during the late summer and early fall as they migrate (Sargent 1968: 388-391). Belugas were hunted from kayaks and whale boats by Caribou Inuit during the historic period of Hudson Bay using harpoons and muskets. In 1810, a Churchill Post-master gave a detailed description of Beluga hunts at Seal River, suggesting that whales were flensed and butchered at rocky outcrops before meat was towed by kayak to the shore (B.42/a/136a). As whale meat is easily stripped from the bone, it is unusual for Beluga bones to make it into archaeological sites unless they are being used for architectural purposes; the skeleton is normally left on the beach where the whale was flensed. A single Beluga vertebral column was observed in a cache that was only 8m away from House I down the escarpment on the south side, however the cache was merely photographed and not excavated (see Figure 23).

Figure 23 Photo of Cache Containing a Beluga Spinal Column, 8m South of House I

Ursus Maritimus (Polar Bear)

A single cranial bone from a Polar bear was recovered. Polar bears can be found in the Arviat region at all times of the year; most commonly in the winter when they hunt ringed and bearded seals on the land-fast ice (Macpherson 1968). Polar bears were not usually hunted by Caribou Inuit, except at incidental meetings (Arima 1984: 448-454).

B. Analysis and Interpretation

Body Part Representation

Caribou and Seals

Ethnographic and historical observations would suggest that caribou and seals were probably the most economically important species to the occupants of House I. Both species are hunted, processed, and consumed in very different ways, which may impact the bones that end up being preserved. By comparing the body parts represented for each of these two species, it may be possible to elucidate specific activities associated with the hunting and processing of each species. Indeed, it was observed during the lab-analysis that certain bones from each species were more or less likely to appear as each unit was analyzed. However, because of the anatomical variation as well as bulk quantity differences between the caribou and seal assemblages, there is some difficulty in quantifying this observation.

In the exploration of body-part representation, the overall number of animals (MNI) represented at the site is of little analytical value. It is more important to calculate the minimum number of elements (MNE) for each skeletal part. However, the MNEs for each of the two assemblages cannot be compared directly because of anatomical differences. For example, a seal has 5 metacarpals on each appendage, whereas a caribou has only one. To standardize MNE, the appropriate measure in this case is minimum number of animal units (MAU) (see Binford 1978; Lyman 1994: 61):

$$MAU = \frac{MNE_e}{\text{number of times } e \text{ occurs in one complete skeleton}}$$

This measure is preferable to other approaches that have been used by zooarchaeologists because there is no reason to assume that any side of the animal was a preferred unit of butchery as was observed by Binford (1978:70) for the Nunamiut. In any case, the caribou assemblage (NISP 268) is approximately half the quantity of the seal assemblage (NISP 563); there is potential for an MNI based approach to over-inflate representation of caribou elements if they occur only on one side incidentally (see Lyman 1994:61).

The MAU values, however, still have to be standardized themselves because the quantity of each assemblage is different. This is usually done by calculating the %MAU, which then represents each MAU according to a scale that is now standardized for comparison between the two assemblages. %MAU is simply calculated as:

$$\%MAU = \frac{(MAU_e)100}{\text{maximum MAU observed in assemblage}}$$

Tables 10 & 11 present the element summaries for House I caribou and seals, with a graphical representation below, which can be used for comparative purposes. There are some significant differences between the two graphs.

Seals

Although there are some anomalously frequent elements (e.g. the atlas) (see Table 10), seal body part representation conforms to a pattern of on-site butchery; whole carcasses of seals were brought into House I and butchered and consumed there. This is supported by a good representation of all cranial, axial and appendicular elements of the seal skeleton. If seals were being processed at a different location before being transported to *Ihatik*, a greater proportion of bones associated with high meat-yielding butchery units would be expected. Lyman et al (1992:535-541), who have created a modified general utility index (MGUI) for *phocids*, rank the ribs and pelvis as being associated with the highest ranking portions. Flippers, especially the forelimbs, yield much less meat and would be more likely to be left behind. The House I pattern is contrary to the *phocid* MGUI; flippers, both fore and hind, rate about the same as ribs and sacral bones in %MAU. This strengthens the interpretation of on-site butchery and processing.

When compared with ethnographic knowledge of Inuit hunting practices, the House I assemblage fits a pattern of winter seal hunting. During the winter, seal carcasses were usually transported whole to the household for a variety of functional and social reasons. Winter sealing was done in frigid temperatures, and it was much easier to transport carcasses by sled to be butchered in warmer sheltered locations. Butchering in exposed conditions would have also increased the likelihood of a carcass freezing before arrival at its destination. In the summer however, seals tended to be butchered on the shore before they were transported (Lyman et al. 1992). Indeed, House I sits on the edge of an escarpment some 20m above the tidal flats, and transporting a whole carcass to the house during the summer would have been an awkward task. In the winter however, the job would be much easier by way of sled. Culturally, it was a traditional practice that women offer the seal a drink of water for its soul by placing fresh water in its mouth and on its belly before butchering it themselves. In the winter, maintenance of this tradition would have required transport of whole seal carcass from the hunting location to the household (see Balikci 1970:77; Boas 1964:154; Lyman et al. 1992:539; Van de Velde 1976:187).

A note-worthy pattern common to Arctic sites where on-site butchery of seals has been identified, is that vertebrae are usually underrepresented (see Leblanc 1994:107, Lyman et al. 1992:546). Lyman et al. (1992:549) hypothesize that as the vertebral elements are "hard-to-manually-deflesh skeletal parts", they are likely to be fed to domestic dogs therefore explaining their regular omission from Arctic sites. An interesting element of the House I seal assemblage is that axial elements are well-represented. Although Lyman et al. (1992:549) have not tested their theory, the normal representation of vertebral elements in the House I seal assemblage adds to the apparent lack of evidence for domestic dogs.

A common pattern among Inuit cultures across the Arctic is that seals were never the exclusive property of the hunter, nor the household that the hunter belonged to. Meat from the hunt was distributed to the community through a complex social network. Different cuts of meat were ranked in their importance, and were distributed according to people's relationship with the household in question (Balikci 1970:77; Boas 1964:154; Lyman et al. 1992:539; Van de Velde 1976).

Steenhoven provides a detailed account of Caribou Inuit seal meat sharing practices at Arviat in 1955 (Steenhoven 1955a: 26). When a hunter killed a Bearded seal, all who were in the vicinity had a right to participate in the flensing, and could keep any part that they removed. The only part that the killer had any right to was the head. Ringed seals however, were the exclusive property of the killer (Steenhoven 1955a: 28).

Table 10 Seal Element Summary

Element (Seal)	NISP	MNE	MAU	%MAU
Cranium	37	6	6.00	0.67
Mandible	12	12	6.00	0.67
Atlas	9	9	9.00	1.00
Axis	4	4	4.00	0.44
Cervical Vertebrae	26	26	5.20	0.58
Thoracic Vertebrae	52	48	3.69	0.41
Lumbar Vertebrae	14	13	2.17	0.24
Ribs	75	57	2.19	0.24
1st Ribs	6	6	3.00	0.33
Scapula	12	11	5.50	0.61
Pelvis	8	8	4.00	0.44
Humerus Proximal	6	6	3.00	0.33
Humerus Distal	6	6	3.00	0.33
Radius Proximal	8	8	4.00	0.44
Radius Distal	8	8	4.00	0.44
Ulna Proximal	6	6	3.00	0.33
Ulna Distal	6	6	3.00	0.33
Metacarpals Proximal	19	5	2.50	0.28
Metacarpals Distal	19	5	2.50	0.28
Carpals	10	4	2.00	0.22
Femur Proximal	13	13	6.50	0.72
Femur Proximal	13	13	6.50	0.72
Tibia Proximal	6	6	3.00	0.33
Tibia Distal	6	6	3.00	0.33
Fibula Proximal	5	5	2.50	0.28
Fibula Distal	5	5	2.50	0.28
Metatarsals Proximal	20	7	3.50	0.39
Metatarsals Distal	20	7	3.50	0.39
Astragalus	5	5	2.50	0.28
Calcaneous	5	5	2.50	0.28

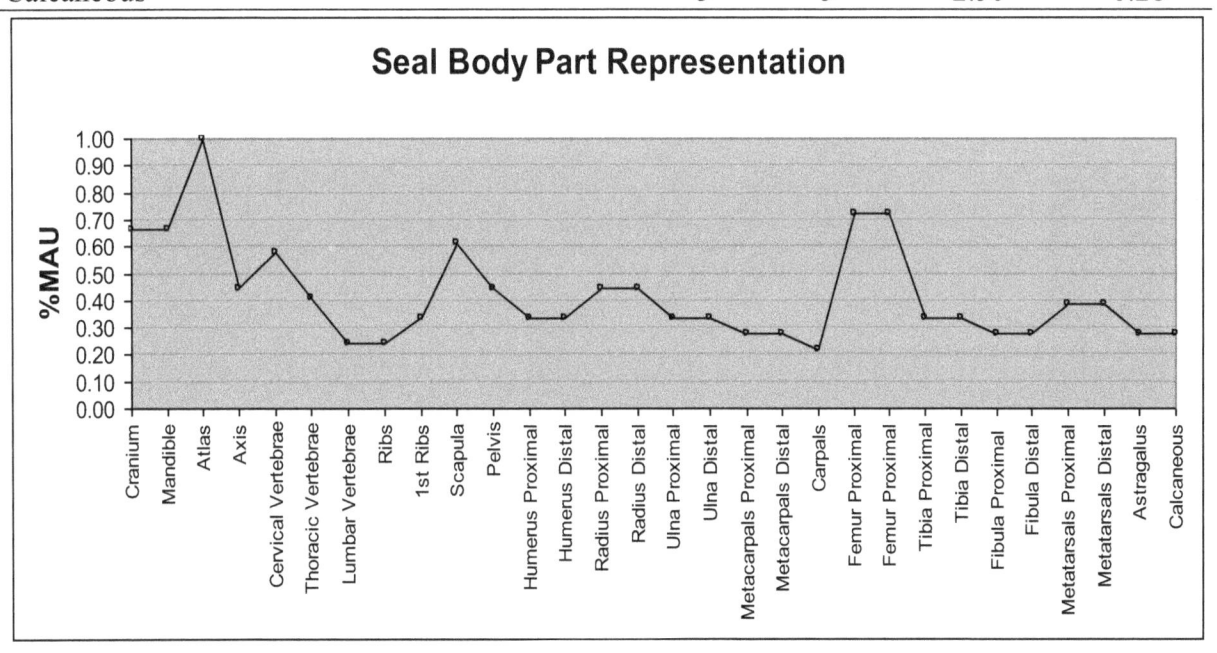

Caribou Inuit Traders of the Kivalliq

Table 11 Caribou Element Summary

Element (Caribou)	NISP	MNE	MAU	%MAU
Antler	1	1	0.5	0.11
Cranium	0	0	0.00	0.00
Mandible	9	9	4.50	1.00
Atlas	0	0	0.00	0.00
Axis	0	0	0.00	0.00
Cervical Vertebrae	1	1	0.20	0.04
Thoracic Vertebrae	17	14	1.01	0.22
Lumbar Vertebrae	0	0	0.00	0.00
Ribs	86	5	0.19	0.04
1st Ribs	1	1	0.50	0.11
Scapula	2	1	0.50	0.11
Pelvis	2	2	1.00	0.22
Humerus Proximal	0	0	0.00	0.00
Humerus Distal	0	0	0.00	0.00
Radius Proximal	5	5	2.50	0.56
Radius Distal	1	1	0.50	0.11
Ulna Proximal	1	1	0.50	0.11
Ulna Distal	0	0	0.00	0.00
Metacarpals Proximal	3	3	1.50	0.33
Metacarpals Distal	0	0	0.00	0.00
Carpals	14	4	2.00	0.44
Femur Proximal	0	0	0.00	0.00
Femur Proximal	0	0	0.00	0.00
Tibia Proximal	3	3	1.50	0.33
Tibia Distal	4	3	1.50	0.33
Fibula Proximal	0	0	0.00	0.00
Fibula Distal	0	0	0.00	0.00
Metatarsals Proximal	4	4	2.00	0.44
Metatarsals Distal	2	2	1.00	0.22
Astragalus	3	3	1.50	0.33
Calcaneous	9	7	3.50	0.78

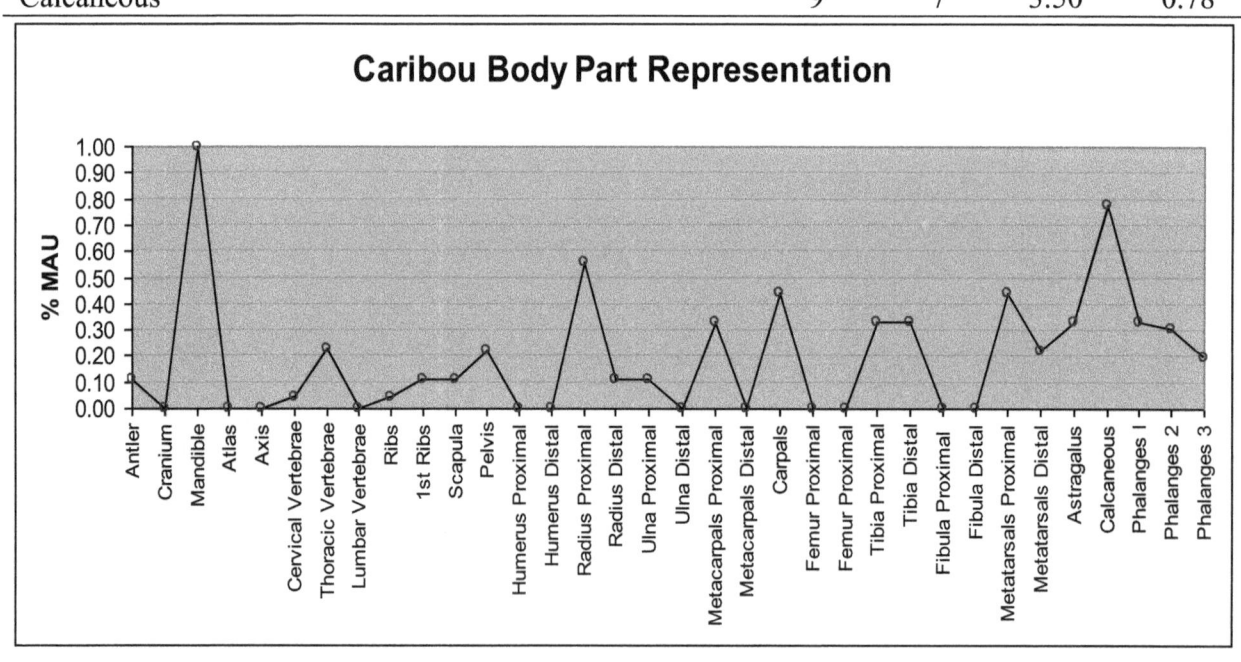

Ownership of meat was immediately transferred to women, once the carcass entered the house, and any further handling, processing, and distribution, was their responsibility (Steenhoven 1955a:28). Families were obliged to offer meat to external requests, but would normally give cuts of lower value (Steenhoven 1955a: 19).

The fact that whole carcasses were staying in House I reveals an important clue about the social conditions at *Ihatik* during the time that House I was occupied; it was possibly an isolated household. The mere presence of the single Bearded seal bone indicates that this was not always the case, but if there were other Inuit households that were normally cohabiting *Ihatik* during the winter occupation of House I, there would probably be a more complex survivorship of small *phocid* bones due to the nature of meat distribution practices. To back up this observation, it can be noted that House I is the only structure of its kind in the vicinity of *Ihatik*.

Caribou

The representation of caribou body parts is difficult to interpret. Many body parts are completely absent, whereas others are disproportionately high. Most interestingly, the pattern is almost the inverse of the caribou meat utility index outlined by Binford (1978:16, 18-20). Skeletal elements from high meat-yielding body parts are mostly absent (see Table 11). This is most noticeable in the complete absence of femurs, and low representation of the scapula and pelvis. In contrast, the parts which are well-represented in House I are very low in their associated utility - especially in the predominance of lower limbs. Binford (1978: 185-447) provides a series of %MAU graphs representing Nunamiut[31] caribou faunal assemblages from a number of site types at various seasons, and documents the associated behaviours that account for the patterns produced. None of the distributions recorded by Binford quite match the assemblage from House I however; it may be that more than one behaviour is accounting for the unique House I distribution.

The Caribou Inuit spent a great deal of the fall hunting and preparing caches of meat for consumption in the winter (Burch 1986:121). The types of meat, and the bones that might get preserved alongside are quite variable, and the exact point in the season is a major consideration across the Arctic (see Mathiassen 1928:202-205). Caribou meat putrefies very quickly, and especially so during the height of the warm season from July to early September. In order for it to be preserved it was removed from the bone which rots very quickly on account of the marrow. The meat was then cut into strips and dried before being cached inside caribou skins (Burch 1986:121). Certain parts of the caribou are not able to be preserved, such as the grease from bones and the marrow which are usually consumed immediately during the summer. As the season gets colder, beyond the beginning of September, it is possible to start caching portions of meat whole, including the bone (Bennett & Rowley 2004: 248-249). Therefore, the bones could represent a combination of behaviours:

1. If the house was occupied during the late summer/early fall, then the bones that arrived in the house for consumption may represent body parts that were more difficult to preserve. This accounts for the high incidence of marrow-rich mandibles, spiral fractured metapodials, and long bone fragments. 'Hoof soup' was a delicacy during this time of year, along with tongues, and grease-rich bones (Rasmussen 1930: 32).

2. If the house was occupied during the winter, then caribou meat would have been accessed from caches spread mostly within a half-day's travel of the house (Bennett & Rowley 2004:247). The bulk of this meat would most likely have consisted of dried meat which would have no 'riders' at all. In some cases, meat that was cached late in the season may have included some bone, but the actual elements may have been highly variable.

Fish Body Part Representation

Within the 959 fish specimens, every single bone from a normal Arctic char skeleton was represented at least once. This is fairly strong evidence that at least some Arctic char were being brought to the house whole. Ethnographically, this seems out of place as fish were normally filleted and dried; this is a process that can cause total bone deletion (Whitridge 1998). There is however some elder knowledge that suggests in special circumstances, namely an overly successful fall fishing season, that fish may be have been cached whole (Bennett & Rowley 2004:252). Another possibility is that the char were being eaten fresh, after being caught in nets. *Ihatik* is a particularly good location to catch char during the summer when nets can be strung out at low tide (Luke Suluk 2006: personal communication).

Diet Breadth

Given the nature of Inuit caching behaviour, it is impossible to construct any sort of diet model that ranks species in economic importance from the House I faunal remains alone. For example, the presence of large quantities of fish bone may suggest that there was an even larger quantity of dried fish that was consumed by the occupants of House I, yet undetected through archaeology. Dried caribou is another good example, along with beluga; there is no way to fully reconstruct how much meat each species actually contributed. As well, there is no way to estimate the importance of European foods, such as flour, sugar, etc., or the ways in

---

[31] The Nunamiut of Alaska are the only other Inuit that lived primarily off of Caribou (Binford 1978)

Caribou Inuit Traders of the Kivalliq

which they supplemented the diet of the occupants of House I. Other Arctic archaeologists seem to concur, and have limited their faunal interpretations to specific behaviours associated with the species present at archaeological sites, rather than definitive statements about diet and food rankings (see Leblanc 1994).

Seasonality

The assortment of evidence regarding seasonality is very complicated and in some cases contradictory. The pattern formed by the seal assemblage certainly points to a winter occupation, where sealing was a major source of food. To support this, it seems quite likely that cached caribou meat was another major food source which would also indicate a winter pattern. Both of these reinforce the architectural conclusion that House I was occupied during a cold season. However, caribou body parts represented at the site could also come from the fall, when higher meat-yielding portions of the carcass were being cached. As well, House I would have had to be occupied during a season where the Bay wasn't frozen over in order to procure the shellfish as they are not cacheable foods. This can be extended to the minimal quantities of bird and rodent bone.

When compiled, I interpret the broad seasonality parameters of the faunal assemblage as suggesting more than one season of occupation. House I is a cold-season structure that was likely constructed in the fall while the ground was not frozen. The house was probably used as a base-camp, while winter stores were hunted and cached at nearby locations, occasionally bringing back meat that was not cached (such as whole fish carcasses, or caribou limbs/mandibles as seen in the faunal assemblage). The occupants then resided in the house during the winter, supplementing their stores with fresh seals which were hunted on the ice and brought back to the house whole.

Regional Comparisons

There are two other coastal sites in the greater vicinity of Arviat that have reported their faunal analyses (see Figure 10).

Nuvuq Point (JhKm-1) has a fairly similar representation of species to that of House I at *Ihatik*. Dawson (2004:32) states that seals dominated the assemblage with 1552 identified specimens accounting for 73% of the faunal assemblage. The body part representation is similar to House I – it would seem that whole seal carcasses were making it to the site. However, while the House I assemblage would suggest that seals were butchered within the structure, the *Nuvuq* assemblage comes from scatters and middens across the site with only a minimal amount of bone being found within the tent-ring structures that were excavated. The caribou assemblage at *Nuvuq* Point is similar to House I in its proportion (%NISP) in the overall faunal assemblage, however the pattern of body part representation is the complete opposite to that observed in House I. Spirally fractured long bone fragments from high-meat yielding portions dominated the assemblage while they are completely absent in House I.

The *Arviaq* Site (JgKl-2) on Sentry Island is also a useful assemblage for comparison. Bertulli (1990:7) reports that the bones analyzed by Oetelaar (1991) were a sample of bones from within a structure that was excavated, not entirely unlike House I, but also from surface collections of nearby scatters. The faunal assemblage was a great deal more fragmented than the House I specimens and over 50% of the *Arviaq* bone was unidentifiable (Oetelaar 1991:2). With the exception of one *canid* bone, the faunal assemblage was exclusively sea mammal. One important difference was that there was an absence of carpals, tarsals, and phalanges at the *Arviaq* site (Oetelaar 1991:5). It can be noted that this is the opposite pattern of House I, where flippers were just as well represented as any other body portion. This may reflect a difference in seasonality, as seasonality has already been suggested as a factor in different butchering patters, or it may also mean that certain cuts of meat were being distributed amongst others living on Sentry Island at the time. The flipper has been pointed out by ethnographers working in other parts of the Arctic, to be of lower preference and is often given to less fortunate or successful households (Bennett & Rowley 2004: 88).

5.3 PART 4: Architectural Discussion

With the Caribou Inuit, semi-subterranean architecture is normally associated with the *qarmat* - a structure type occasionally used by Inuit for temporary shelter during the transition between the seasons when it is not warm enough for summer tents, yet the snow is not suitable for the construction of snow houses (Birket-Smith 1929:84). This practice generally occurred for no more than a couple of weeks in late-October to early-November, and then again in early-June. *Qarmat* in general are ovate, slightly depressed, and have walls composed of sod blocks, large stones, or snow blocks (Lee & Reinhardt 2003:52). The roofs of these structures usually consisted of an old tent skin draped across the opposing walls. *Qarmat* are associated with difficult times for Inuit, when weather conditions hinder travel, when game is scarce, and stores are low or inaccessible. Maintaining a *qarmat* was a constant struggle to patch holes created by heavy rain and winds (Bennet & Rowley 2004:228-232).

Although House I most closely resembles a *qarmat* in terms of known Caribou Inuit categories of dwelling, there are certain properties of its architecture and material assemblage that suggest a completely different pattern. The cultural materials removed from the house are not indicative of a temporary occupation, but rather a greater degree of sedentism extending into several seasons. In their comparison of Inuit architecture across the Arctic, Lee and Reinhardt's (2003:160) tabulation of architectural types would place House I as a primary winter residence on the grounds that the primary chamber is well-excavated with a raised entrance passage, and there is clear evidence of a hearth. As well, the dimensions of the house, 4m at the narrowest, make it unlikely that it would have simply been covered with an old tent skin draped between the 50 cm high walls.

Considering the available materials along with Inuit architectural solutions from across the Arctic, it is possible to narrow the nature of the super-structure to a number of possibilities. As with some *qarmats*, the walls of the structure could have been made from snow blocks that were cut and then stacked on top of the perimeter. Once the blocks melted away, they would have left no evidence of their existence which matches the results of the excavation. However, there are a couple of technical issues which disqualify this possibility. First of all, most *qarmats* that use snow block walls are fairly small because the roof itself is simply a tent skin that stretches across the opening (see Friesen & Stewart 2004). Given the size of the structure, it would have been impossible to do this without an elaborate network of cross beams that would cover the 32 m² area. Such a structure would have been difficult to support with snow block walls. Even in snow houses (*iglus*), snow blocks had to form a perimeter that was as round as possible if the house was to be used for any period of time due to the fact that snow blocks settle and change shape very quickly, and cannot support very much weight (Bennett and Rowley 2004:237; Boas 1964:132-133; Mathiassen 1928:123-129). As well, suitable snow for cutting snow blocks only forms under certain conditions which take time to develop (Birket-Smith 1929a: 6). Even if House I was built specifically for winter use, it can be deduced that the actual excavation and construction of the base must have taken place during a season when the ground wasn't frozen, which precludes the use of snow blocks. In other parts of the Arctic, temporary shelters were occasionally built using ice blocks instead of snow. However, such structures were strictly temporary as they were much colder than snow houses. They were built when there was not enough snow, but the tops of lakes or ponds had frozen just a little so that blocks could be broken out of it. Neither strategy seems suitable for more permanent structures such as House I (Mathiassen 1928:138-139).

For the Inuit in general, skin tents are usually synonymous with summer life. In the Caribou Inuit area however, it has been documented that tents were sometimes used in the winter as well (Bennett and Rowley 2004: 244-245). Such tents had a double liner and the middle was stuffed with moss and heather for insulation. A small space was left in the side of the tent through with a pipe would be raised to act as a chimney (see Plate 9). Sometimes, snow blocks were piled along the outside of the tent to hold it down and provide further insulation. Historical examples include Augustus, a Padlirmiut Homeguard, who, when working at Churchill, would live in a tent throughout the winter (B.42/a/145). Augustus also lived in a winter tent with Ullebuk when they worked together in Ungava, Quebec during the 1830s (Rich 1953: 370-371) Another example is Qiqut, the Ahiarmiut trader, who lived the entire winter in a tent

Figure 24 Richard Harrington's Photo of an Ahiarmiut Tent at Padlei

(Harrington in Bennett & Rowley 2004:244)

that was so large that he used two stoves to heat it, and could keep his kayak and all of his trade goods inside (see Chapter 4) (Lyons 2007: 37-38). Typical Caribou Inuit tents are conical with a circular base, but Birket-Smith (1929a:86) interviewed some Inuit near Arviat who remember building longer ovate tents by using *komatik* runners as cross beams and ridge poles. Steenhoven photographed this tent type in 1955 (see Figure 25). There are several bilobate and ovate summer tent ring features at the *Ihatik* site which are of comparable size to House I, so this technique could easily have been used to cover House I (see Figure 26).

Figure 25 G. Steenhoven's Photo of an Elongated AhiarmiutTent At Ennadai Lake, 1955

(Steenhoven in Csonka 1995)

Although there is no conclusive evidence regarding the super-structure of House I, it seems most likely that it would have been covered with a tent given the range of possibilities. This explains the absence of architectural features such as post-holes, the absence of architectural materials in the fill, and fits very nicely with ethnographic observations of Caribou Inuit winter tent use. The ovate nature of the structure seems to be most suitably covered by a tent; it falls within the range of tent-ring sizes and shapes at *Ihatik*, even if the semi-subterranean architecture sets it apart.

Figure 26 Photo of an *Ihatik* Tent Ring of Comparable Dimensions to House I

5.3 PART 5: Activity Areas

Although there were definite concentrations of artifacts, activity areas were not easily defined on the basis of architecture. For example, Thule semi-subterranean houses typically have a flagstone floor with an elevated sleeping platform; no such structure was delineated in House I (see Mary-Rousellière 1979:60-61). Sleeping areas are usually built on areas that are flat. They consist of layers of skins and Arctic heather. In order to keep everything in one place, the sleeping area is usually enclosed with a boundary of either wood or stone (Bennett & Rowley 2004: 243-245; Birket-Smith 1929a: 87). In the summer tents, it can be seen that the skins and heather were held in using pieces of wood, such as an old *komatik* runner (see Figure 14) (Birket-Smith 1929a: 86). Using the criteria that sleeping areas have to be relatively flat (i.e. free of large rocks), and that they are to be found along the walls of houses rather than in the middle, then there are only two areas in House I that could have served that purpose. The first is the northeast corner, and the second is the southwest. The southwest area has the highest potential because there does appear to be a line of rocks that could have served the purpose of holding everything in. Alternatively, the northeast corner could have been enclosed by rocks that were then shifted, or more likely wooden barriers that were later salvaged. When elders at the Nunavut Elder's Council were shown pictures of the house during a presentation in Arviat in the summer of 2006 by Dr. Peter Dawson, the unanimous response was that two families would have lived in House I based primarily on its shape and size. As a result it is entirely possible that both areas were sleeping areas.

In the southeast quarter, there was a concentration of rocks that were associated with patches of burned blubber and seal oil (see Figure 18). As well there was a great deal of charred wood and bone fragments that were in this location and the units adjacent. The area has been interpreted as a cooking and food preparation area. Food preparation would likely have been done through both the qulliq seal oil lamps as well as fires of arctic willow which is a classic Caribou Inuit pattern (Birket-Smith 1929a: 87-90). Other artifacts associated with this area included the slip-lid container fragments, the file (possibly used as a strike-a–light), and the match box lid (see Figure 18). Indeed, 73% of the entire faunal sample was recovered along the southwest wall, in close association with the 'cooking area' (see Figure 18). It is possible the South half of House I functioned as a cooking/sleeping area.

In general, most of the artifacts and faunal materials were found in clusters, or along the inner walls of the house (see Figure 18). Concentrations of nails, along with wood debitage and other construction related artifacts suggest related activities in the western-central part of the North half of House I. Artifacts were found in concentrations, along the walls especially, which may demarcate these as sitting/working areas. However, this is also suggestive of the activity of cleaning the space in the middle by simply pushing garbage up against the sides. The area immediately inside the entrance passage had very low numbers of artifacts and faunal materials, which is a good indication that the area was kept clear of materials and activity (see Figure 18). If House I is a cold-season dwelling, as it has been interpreted, then it is likely that the floor would have been covered with willows and moss for insulation during most of the time that it was occupied (see Bennett & Rowley 2004; 244-245). The insulation layers may have been periodically replaced, or simply burned for fuel once the material was no longer needed for insulation; both possibilities would further obscure any spatial patterns of artifacts that can be associated with activities.

Chapter 6 – Discussions and Conclusion

6.1 House I Discussion

House I is an anomaly that is not easily reconciled with the ethnographic and archaeological depiction of Caribou Inuit culture. In general, Caribou Inuit were highly mobile due to their subsistence strategy; they lived in temporary tents during brief summer occupations of the coast, they travelled inland by August to participate in the most important event of the year, the fall caribou hunt, and they remained the winter at inland locations in close proximity to their caches of caribou meat (see Chapter 3) (Arima 1984; Burch 1986: 115-116; Birket-Smith 1929a; Rasmussen 1930: 10-11). In contrast, House I is suggestive of an Inuit multi-season occupation of a single structure at a coastal location, with a reliance on sea-mammal hunting during the cold season. Why is House I so different, and what does it represent? This question must be assessed in terms of the history and the types of people that were living in the Kivalliq during the mid-late 1800s.

The most revealing archaeological feature of House I may be its very location. The Arviat area would have been a major intersection for Inuit travellers during the 1800s; especially during the period when Churchill was the only direct venue for European trade. Arviat is in the direct path of almost anyone in the Kivalliq travelling to Churchill, either along the coast, or from the interior (see Figure 1 & 2). The Maguse River system was a major route of travel that eventually connects from Hudson Bay into Hikoligjuaq Lake, which was the axis of Padlirmiut, Ahiarmiut, and Harvaqtormiut territory, and the centre of interaction between those groups (Birket-Smith 1929a: 64-66, 130-132, 134-136; Rasmussen 1930). Through Hikoligjuaq Lake and the Kazan River system, Arviat is also connected to Baker Lake, the Thelon system, and therefore *Akilineq* and beyond (see Figure 7). In addition, Arviat was also the southernmost Inuit community that would have been encountered by Inuit travelling along the coast from northern locations, such as Marble Island and Wager Bay, before the final stretch to Churchill. As well as an intersection for travellers, the Arviat area was also frequented by Padlirmiut living traditional patterns of subsistence during the summer (Birket-Smith 1929a: 64-66). Travelling down the Maguse River, the Padlirmiut would arrive early in the spring, spending the summer at large aggregation sites including *Ihatik* (Louie Angalik in Dawson et al 2006: 18-19). Arviat was the single-most critical junction between the Kivalliq and Churchill during the 1800s, and House I was cleverly perched in the perfect location to keep an eye on the entire area (see Figure 10-13).

An Inuk trader using Austin Island as a location to intercept a large cross section of the Caribou Inuit in the late 1800s would not have been likely to use the *Ihatik* site in the same ways that traditional Padlirmiut did. House I is more than a little reminiscent of Qiqut's tent; the architecture meets the same needs, and it probably served a similar function to that of European trade posts (see Chapter 4). House I was possibly used as a semi-permanent structure which other Inuit, also travelling large distances, could reliably arrive at to trade in a variety of seasons that were suitable for travel and their hunting schedule. The large size of House I, like Qiqut's tent, probably accommodated the need for extended residence along with the storage of trade products. Padlirmiut Elders at Arviat suggested that one of the reasons for the size of Qiqut's tent was that he used it to extend hospitality and accommodate travellers as a part of the trading process (Lyons 2007: 37-38). House I probably functioned in a similar manner.

On the surface, it would seem strange to suggest that House I was used by an Inuit trading family if it was occupied during seasons when other Inuit were not normally present at *Ihatik*; indeed I have suggested that the pattern of seal bones in House I may indicate that House I was predominantly an isolated household. It would seem more sensible to locate such a facility in close proximity to large numbers of Caribou Inuit, who would have been located at inland lakes during the winter. However, there are at least three functional advantages to operating a winter camp at *Ihatik* if trade was the primary consideration:

1. Transportation Costs

Ihatik would have been within the sled range of Padlirmiut wintering at the Maguse and Hikoligjuaq Lakes. Winter probably would have been the ideal time to conduct trade, as Caribou Inuit would have been less occupied with the fall caribou hunt, and once the winter stores had been stockpiled they would have been in a better position to assess what they could trade. In addition, *Ihatik* is essentially a multi-season site even if it was primarily occupied in the summer. The most common features at *Ihatik* were summer tent rings, but this was followed closely by various meat caches (see Table 7). The fact that caches were being placed at *Ihatik* during its summer occupation indicates that Padlirmiut were travelling to *Ihatik* during the winter, if only to retrieve the cached foods.

Transporting large quantities of trade goods to *Ihatik*, from Churchill in the late-summer, would certainly have been done using boats. Moving those products inland, however, may have been more problematic. The sample assemblage of faunal remains had almost no evidence to suggest the presence of domestic dogs, which would certainly have been used if inland transportation had been a concern for those living in House I. This pattern makes sense when it is considered that Coastal Homeguards appear to have travelled primarily by boat; in the case of William Ullebuk, he even owned and operated a coastal schooner. Conducting trade from *Ihatik* removes a significant part

Caribou Inuit Traders of the Kivalliq

of the transportation costs from the trading party by transferring it to those who travelled there to trade.

2. Intercepting Travellers

Spring was the major time of travel for Caribou Inuit that were going to Churchill whether they were Homeguards or occasional traders. Such Inuit would generally travel by sled or boat to Churchill along the coastal route (Chapter 4). For a Homeguard, being at *Ihatik* before anyone had the chance to make that trip would have allowed them to intercept any travellers, offering them the advantage of significantly shortening their journey. This would have been particularly appealing if travel conditions were poor.

3. Economic Independence

Returning to the North to participate in the fall caribou hunt was a major scheduling concern for Coastal Homeguards that spent the majority of the summer hunting seals at Seal River. This would be a risky strategy when it is considered that the success of the fall caribou hunt was crucial to survival through the winter. If the journey back to northern wintering grounds was hindered by any circumstance such as weather or disease, the results could be disastrous. At the very least, Homeguards would have to spend the winter trading their European items directly for food under these cirumstances. Hunting seals at *Ihatik* throughout the winter, though not normally practiced, would have balanced this situation and allowed a Homeguard family to be more economically independent. This would have increased their power in trade exchanges.

House I and the Caribou Inuit Traders of the Kivalliq

Any of the coastal Homeguards of the mid to late 1800s, which have been profiled in Chapter 4, could have been likely to have occupied House I. William Ullebuk is a particularly strong possibility, as he would have been intimately familiar with the techniques of winter seal hunting through his interaction with Inuit whilst travelling with John Rae. As well, he probably spent a great deal of his childhood in Ungava, Quebec where seal hunting is regularly practiced (see Rich 1953: 373-374).

With the view that an Inuit trader occupied House I, the artifact assemblage becomes even more meaningful. With the exception of the copper and bead ornament, the European artifacts seem to have served strictly utilitarian purposes, and none of the HBC items themselves imply activities that would account for the unique architectural and subsistence pattern of House I. Although Homeguards had dramatically changed subsistence patterns, using strategies such as that represented by House I in order to traffic European trade items, their own application of those items seem to have been supplemental at best.

Perhaps most importantly, House I is a record of an extended family – the significant social unit in Caribou Inuit society. The architecture alone suggests the accommodation of family sized social unit. The patterns of artifacts and faunal materials imply a number of activities which, if taken alone, represent different genders. The ground stone ulu, for example, is an artifact type that is almost exclusively associated with females, where as the construction debris would normally be associated with male activities.

If a specific individual, suppose William Ullebuk, occupied House I, then it can be seen that he depended upon his family. Whilst awaiting other Caribou Inuit who wished to trade, he probably hunted seals with his sons and brothers, bringing the carcasses back to be butchered by his daughters, mother, and wife(s). He would have travelled to caches of caribou meat and char that they had collectively hunted and prepared for storage in the fall. The clothes he wore and the skin of his kayak, would have been prepared and sewn by members of his family at House I, as evidenced by the ring of pegs. House I had no architectural partition, or separate structure from which trade was conducted; when other Caribou Inuit came to House I to trade, they likely did so in the company and presence of the entire family, in a similar fashion to Qiqut's tent. This calls into question the assumption that the trade of European goods would have been the explicit domain of a male trader such as William Ullebuk. 'William Ullebuk' may be the name that appears in the HBC trade books, but the very lifestyle of being a Homeguard demanded cooperation and interdependence of the extended family in a similar fashion to traditional life; the importance of this social unit, while largely absent in historical documentation, is observed archaeologically.

6.2 Conclusions and Directions for Future Research

Theoretical

The socio-cultural transition of the Caribou Inuit from a traditional economy to a larger world economic system during the colonial period of Hudson Bay might be approached using world systems theory. World system theory examines the ways that European capitalism incorporated various indigenous economies, forming a single global system; colonial countries are conceptualized as core areas that annexed peripheral areas containing indigenous cultures, in order to acquire labour and raw materials (Wallerstein 1974, 1980). World system theory assumes that Indigenous peoples are lured into participating in European economies via trade, which offers them technologies that they could not previously access (Cabak & Loring 2000: 2; Dunaway 1994). From a very broad perspective, this would accurately describe the incorporation of the Caribou Inuit into a world economic system. The Kivalliq could be defined as a periphery, used by the core area to acquire raw materials such as furs, sea mammal oil, baleen, and ivory, in exchange for metal implements and guns. At the beginning of the colonial period, the Caribou Inuit lived autonomous traditional lives, and by the 1960s, they lived in Euro-Canadian towns in a relationship of dependency on the Canadian Government (Williamson 1974: 7-11). In this very broad sense, the case of the Caribou Inuit could easily be subsumed into a large explanatory theory such as world systems analysis.

However, as documented in this study, the incorporation of European trade into Caribou Inuit society was not a simple process; it took hundreds of years, and included multiple generations of Caribou Inuit who lived their entire lives in an autonomous state, able to choose the extent to which they wanted to participate in the world economy. As discussed in Chapter 4, the lure of highly functional technologies such as muskets and metal knives was not enough to draw the Caribou Inuit into a relationship of dependency, even when trade was brought to them by the HBC between the years 1717-1790. When the HBC ceased the trade sloops in 1790, the general response of the Caribou Inuit appears to have been ambivalence; a very small number of Caribou Inuit actually made the journey to Churchill in order to continue trading. These events contradict the basic premise of world system theory, and it was eventually Caribou Inuit, not Europeans, that shaped the development of Caribou Inuit culture during the historic period.

Other anthropologists and archaeologists have had difficulty in applying world systems analysis to Arctic contexts. For example, T. Max Friesen originally used world systems analysis as an explanatory framework for the historic period of the Mackenzie Delta Inuvialuit at Herschel Island, Yukon Territory (Friesen 1996). In his dissertation, the application of world system theory also included some elements of cultural ecology, which appropriately offset the concepts of 'core' and 'periphery'. Incorporation of the Inuvialuit into a world economy was explained by the concept of 'preciosities', which were trade items that were highly valued by the Inuvialuit; Inuvialuit were drawn into participation by the need to procure preciosities, thus making the economic shift quite rapid with immediate social reorganization due to the emergence of social differentiation (Friesen 1996:197-277).

Friesen has since revisited the issue of Inuvialuit cultural change in the historic period with an article that describes the journals of Isaac O. Stringer, an Anglican Missionary, who vividly described Inuvialuit life in the 1890s at Kitigaaryuit, North West Territories (Friesen 2004). Stringer's journals provided Friesen with a high-resolution examination of day-to-day life at Kitigaaryuit over the period of a decade (Friesen 2004: 224-226, 233). Stringer depicts an Inuvialuit population that were in possession of a large quantity of European trade items, yet traditional technologies and subsistence, primarily Beluga hunting with kayaks and harpoons was still the central aspect of Inuvialuit life (Friesen 2004: 233-234). The Kitigaaryuit area, seems to have been a very similar situation to that of the Kivalliq; there were multiple groups at Kitigaaryuit, including the Kitigagzyoomioot,

Chapter 6 – Discussions and Conclusion

the Kuwhchamioot, the Tchenegagmioot, and the Noonatagmioout[32]. Each of these groups participated in European trade in very different ways to eachother (Friesen 2004: 231-232). Over the course of Stringer's observations, there were several large-scale demographic changes due to epidemics of various diseases. These epidemics nearly obliterated some groups, and it was the tragic consequence of these events that prevented the Inuvialuit from continuing traditional hunting practices, turning instead to a greater dependency on the Anglican Church. Friesen concludes that rather than the introduction of the European economy, the main catalysts for change in Inuvialuit culture were the Inuvialuit themselves, local demographic shifts, and the effect of epidemics (Friesen 2004: 234-235).

Melanie Cabak and Stephen Loring also discuss the applicability of world-system theory in their examination of the incorporation of Labrador Inuit into the global economic system (Cabak & Loring 2000). In their excavation of the Inuit village site of Nain, Cabak & Loring document a steady increase of Inuit consumption of fine European stamped ceramics; indeed, world systems theory predicts the increased consumption of such items, or preciosities (Cabak & Loring 2000: 11-15). However, Cabak & Loring demonstrate that the popularity of the ceramics was linked to the continuation of traditional food ways rather than a shift towards consumerism. Similar to the European items recovered from House I, ceramics at Nain were used to supplement traditional activities. Cabak & Loring conclude by suggesting that world systems theory does not appropriately account for the agency of indigenous cultures in shaping the economic transitions that occurred in the colonial period (Cabak & Loring 2000: 31).

Another recent example is Marc Stevenson's examination of cultural change and continuity of Inuit interacting with whalers at Cumberland Sound, Baffin Island during the late 1800s (Stevenson 1997). Stevenson does not specifically mention world systems theory, but his conclusions are very similar to those of Cabak, Friesen, and Loring. Stevenson shows that Inuit rapidly incorporated European technologies such as whale boats and firearms, but that their application of those items was supplemental to traditional subsistence patterns. The economic transition in Cumberland Sound Inuit society, during interaction with whalers, was governed not by consumerism but by indigenous social organization and concepts of leadership (Stevenson 1997: 139-140).

In examining each of the examples from Cumberland Sound, the Kivalliq, Labrador, and the Mackenzie Delta, it is apparent that each of the Inuit cultures underwent socio-cultural changes related to the introduction of European trade, but that the primary agents in shaping the process were the Inuit themselves.

---

[32] The Kitigagzyoomioot, the Kuwhchamioot, the Tchenegagmioot are all local sub-groupings of the Inuvialuit. The Noonatagmioout, elsewhere referred to as 'Nunamiut' are a migrant group of Alaskan Inupiat (Friesen 2004: 231-232).

This fact accounts for the diversity of Inuit experiences across the Arctic in the historic period. Rather than broad generalizing theories, such as world systems analysis, applications of theory by Arctic archaeologists must take into account local histories; Caribou Inuit society can only be examined using a theoretical framework that has been developed, in part, by a consideration of the Caribou Inuit themselves.

Regarding the process of Caribou Inuit economic and cultural transition in the early historic period, this study can offer at least one conclusion; the introduction of European trade did not affect Caribou Inuit individuals equally, and they participated in different ways. Culture change then cannot be conceptualized as the reaction of a consolidated entity to external stimulus - in this case, the Caribou Inuit culture to European trade. For example, in Chapter 4, the reactions of Caribou Inuit to the cessation of trade sloops in 1790 were grouped into three categories: the bulk population who did not travel to Churchill, those who occasionally travelled to Churchill, and those who incorporated Churchill into subsistence and are referred to as 'Homeguards'. In reality, even these categories are artificial, as there are significant differences between individuals who have been loosely thrown into one or another. Indeed, the very location of House I was probably well thought out, before construction, so that its occupants would be well placed to intercept a variety of Caribou Inuit that were inclined to participate in trade in very different ways. Participation in European trade was a continuum, and the extent to which it occurred for individuals probably depended upon the extended families of which they were a part.

The primary agents for social change in Caribou Inuit culture were the extended families that pursued a lifestyle as Homeguards, or intermediaries in trade. This adds an element of unpredictability to the examination of Caribou Inuit cultural transition as a process. After all, it is only a select number of families that could be characterized as Homeguards. The motives and benefits behind the decision to incorporate European trade at such a high level probably lie within the realm of family politics, due to the social organization of the Caribou Inuit; it is unlikely that this was done in order to embrace a world economy, but rather to use European trade to benefit and perpetuate the family's position in existing social structures and trade networks. The notion that they were agents of a 'core area' in extracting labour and raw materials from the Kivalliq as a 'peripheral area' may have been totally absurd to a Caribou Inuit trade family.

As this study studies a fairly recent time period, it has drawn upon archival and oral history in addition to archaeology. The combination of these sources has allowed for a high-resolution perspective of the historic period of the Kivalliq. This resolution of data is generally unavailable to research questions that are prehistoric in nature, such as the origins of Caribou Inuit culture.

Methodological

A methodological shortcoming, intrinsic to the study but irreversible at this point in time, can be found in the application of Elder knowledge from the Arviat Oral History Project. During the summer of 2007, I provided Natasha Lyons with the names of individuals who figure prominently in the historical literature, such as the Ullebuks, Qaqami, and Qiqut. The Padlirmiut Elders were then asked if they recognized the names, and if they knew any stories about those individuals. In some cases, this approach was met with a great deal of success and a lot of information about those individuals, which would not have been apparent in the historical documentation, was incorporated into this study. However, this approach has also replicated the bias of the historical literature by positing such individuals as prominent in the first place; the Elders were not asked about people who did not appear in the history.

I would suggest, as a future direction for the Arviat Oral History Project, a more explicit examination and reconstruction of the families that the Inuit traders profiled in this study were a part of. For example, of William Ullebuk it could be asked: "How many sons and daughters did he have? What were their names? Who were his wives and where were they from? When did his mother die? How many siblings did he have? Was he an *Angakok*? Were any of his family members *Angakut*?". Because of the importance of the extended family in the decision making process, it is equally important to examine the individuals to which William Ullebuk was connected.

This study demonstrates that combining archival history with oral history and archaeology is a productive methodology. By integrating these approaches, it has been possible to conduct a more complete examination of Caribou Inuit cultural transitions in the historic period; it would seem that there are many complex social and historical processes, of which this study has only scratched the surface. The continued application of this methodology in the Caribou Inuit area should be encouraged, with the intent that it may eventually be used as a powerful analogy for examining the development of Historic Inuit cultures from a common Thule ancestral base in other areas of the Canadian Arctic, as well, as this process is not well understood.

Bibliographic References

Arima, E. Y.
1975 *A Contextual Study of the Caribou Eskimo Kayak*. National Museum of Man Mercury Series 25. National Musuems of Canada, Ottawa.

―

1984 Caribou Eskimo. In *Arctic*, edited by D. Damas, pp. 447-463. Handbook of North American Indians. vol. 5. Smithsonian Institution, Washington.

Balikci, A.
1970 *The Netsilik Eskimo*. The Natural History Press, Garden City.

Banfield, A. W. F.
1974 *Mammals of Canada*. University of Toronto Press, Toronto.

Barr, W.

1991 *Back Form the Brink: The Road to Muskox Conservation in the Northwest Teriitories*. Komatik Series Number 3. Arctic Institute of North America, Calgary.

―

1999 *Searching for Franklin: The Land Arctic Searching Expedition, 1855*. Third Series Number I. Hakluyt Society, London.

Beattie, O. and J. Geiger
1993 *Dead Silence: The Greatest Mystery in Arctic Discovery*. Viking, Toronto.

Bennett, J. and S. Rowley
2004 *Uqalurait: An Oral History of Nunavut*. McGill-Queens Native and Northern Series. McGill-Queens University Press, Montreal.

Bertulli, M.
1990 *Arviat Archaeology Project: Report of the 1989 Field Season*. Permit 89-663. Prince of Wales Northern Heritage Centre.

Binford, L. R.
1978 *Nunamiut Ethnoarchaeology*. Academic Press, New York.

Birket-Smith, K.
1929a *The Caribou Eskimos: Material and Social Life and Their Cultural Position - Descriptive Part*. Report of the Fifth Thule Expedition 1921-24 V. AMS Press, New York.

―

1929b *The Caribou Eskimos: Material and Social Life and Their Cultural Position - Analytical Part*. Report of the Fifth Thule Expedition 1921-1924 V. AMS Press, Copenhagen.

Bitting, A. W.
1937 *Appertizing or the Art of Canning; Its History and Development*. The Trade Pressroom, San Fransisco.

Boas, F.
1964 *The Central Eskimo*. University of Nebraska Press, Lincoln.

Burch, E. S. Jr.
1978 Caribou Eskimo Origins: An Old Problem Reconsidered. *Arctic Anthropology* 15(1):1-38.

―

1979 The Thule-historic Eskimo Transition on the west Coast of Hudson Bay. In *Thule Eskimo Culture: An anthropological Retrospective*, edited by A.P. McCartney, pp. 189-211. vol. 88. National Museums of Canada, Ottawa.

―

1986 The Caribou Inuit. In *Native Peoples: the Canadian Experience*, edited by R. B. Morrison and C. Roderick. McLelland & Stewart, Toronto.

―

1988 Knud Rasmussen and the "Original" Inland Eskimos of Southern Keewatin. *Inuit Studies* 12(1):81-100.

―

1995 The Caribou Inuit. In *Native Peoples: The Canadian Experience.*, edited by R. B. Morrison and C. R. Wilson, pp. 115-142. 2nd ed. Oxford University Press, Toronto.

Cabak, M. and S. Loring
2000 "A Set of Very Fair Cups and Saucers": Stamped Ceramics as an Example of Inuit Incorporation. *International Journal of Historical Archaeology* 4(1):1-34.

Clark, B. L.
1975 *The Development of the Caribou Eskimo Culture*. Master of Arts, Memorial University of Newfoundland.

Cooch, F. G.
　1968　Birds of Hudson Bay. In *Science, History and Hudson Bay*, edited by C. S. Beals. vol. I. Department of Energy, Mines and Resources, Ottawa.

Cooke, A. and C. Holland
　1978　*The Exploration of Northern Canada: 500 to 1920, a Chronology*. The Arctic History Press, Toronto.

Csonka, Y.
　1994　Intermédiaires au Long Cours: les Relations entre Inuit du Caribou et Inuit du Cuivre au Début du XXe Siècle. *Inuit Studies* 18(1-2):21-47.

　—
　1995　Les Ahiarmiut. Éditions Victor Attenger, Neuchâtel.

Damas, D.
　1968　The Eskimo. In *Science, History, and Hudson Bay*, edited by C. S. Beals, pp. 141-171. vol. I. Department of Mining and Natural Resources, Ottawa.

　—
　1988　The Contac-traditional Horizon of the Central Arctic: Reassessment of a Concept and Rexamination of and Era. *Arctic Anthropology* 25(2):101-138.

Davies, K. G. and A. M. Johnson (editors)
　1965　*Letters from Hudson Bay 1703-40. 25*. Hudson's Bay Record Society, London.

Davis, A.
　1967　*Package and Print*. Faber and Faber, London.

Dawson, P. C.
　2005　A Final Report on Archaeological Fieldwork Undertaken Near the Community of Arviat, Nunavut, During the Summer of 2003 (Permits 03-6A & 3-18A), Nunavut Government.

Dawson, P. C., N. Lyons, D. Uluadluak, L. Angalik, J. Karatek, R. Manik, and M. Kalluak
　2006　Traditional Use and Oral History of the Maguse Lake Region: 2006. University of Calgary.

Dawson, P. C., M. D. Walls and L. Suluk
　2007　A Final Report of Archaeological Research Undertaken on Austin Island, Nunavut, Under Archaeologists Permit 2006-015A. Nunavut Government.

DeAngelis, H. and J. Kleman
　2005　Paleo-ice Streams in the Northern Keewatin Sector of the Laurentide Ice Sheet. *Annals of Glaciology Society* 42(1):1235-144.

Dorais, L.J.
　1990　*Inuit Languages and Dialects*. Arctic College, Iqaluit.

　—
　1993　*From Magic Words to Word Processing: A History of the Inuit Language*. Arctic College, Iqaluit

Dunaway, W. A.
　1994　The Southern Fur Trade and the Incorporation of Southern Appalachia into the World-Economy, 1690-1763. *Review* 17(2): 215-242.

Fossett, R.
　2001　*In Order to Live Untroubled: Inuit of the Central Arctic, 1550 to 1940*. The University of Manitoba Press, Winnipeg.

Franklin, J.
　1823　*Narrative of a Journey to the Shores of the Polar See in the years 1819-22*, London.

　—
　1928　*Narrative of a Second Expedition to the shores of the Polar Sea in the Years 1825, 1826, and 1827*. London.

Freeman, N. G. and T. S. Murty
　1976　Numerical Modeling of Tides in Hudson Bay. *Journal of the Fisheries Research Board of Canada* 33(10):2345-2361.

Friesen, T.M.
　1996　*Periphery as Centre: Long-term Patterns of Intersocietal Interaction on Herschel Island, Northern Yukon Territory*. McGill University.

　—
　2004　Kitigaaryuit: A Portrait of the Mackenzie Inuit in the 1890s, Based on the Journals of Isaac O. Stringer. *Arctic Anthropology* 43(2): 222-237.

Friesen, T. M. and A. M. Stewart
　2004　Variation in Subsistence Among Inland Inuit: Zooarchaeology of Two Sites on the Kazan River, Nunavut. *Canadian Journal of Archaeology* 28:32-50.

Gagnon, A. S. and W. A. Gough
    2002   Hydro-Climatic Trends in the Hudson Bay Region, Canada. *Canadian Water Resources Journal* 27(3):245-262.

Gates, C.
    1989   Kaminuriak Herd. In *People and Caribou in the Northwest Territories*, edited by E. Hall. Department of Renewable Resources, Ottawa.

Glover, R.
    1958   Editor's Introduction. In *A Journey from Prince of Wales's Fort in Hudson's Bay to the Northern Ocean*, edited by R. Glover, pp. vii-xliii. Macmillan Company of Canada, Toronto.

Gordon, B. C
    1974   *Of Men and Herds in Barrenlands Prehistory*, University of Calgary.

―

    1988   Nadlok and its Unusual Antler Dwellings. *Arctic* 41(2):160-161.

―

    1996   *People of Sunlight, People of Starlight*. Mercury Series Archaeological Survey of Canada 154. Canadian Museum of Civilization, Ottawa.

―

    2005   8000 Years of Caribou and Human Seasonal Migration in the Canadian Barrenlands. *Rangifer* (16):155-162.

Graham, A.
    1969   *Andrew Graham's Observations on Hudson's Bay 1767-91. Publications of Hudson's Bay Record Society XXVII*. Hudson's Bay Record Society, London.

Grayson, D. K.
    1979   On the Quantification of Vertebrate Archaeofaunas. In *Advances in Archaeological Method and Theory*, edited by M. B. Schiffer. vol. 2. Academic Press, New Tork.

Harp, E.
    1961   *The Archaeology of the Lower and Middle Thelon, Northwest Territories*. Technical Papers 8. Arctic Institute of North America, Calgary.

Harper, F.
    1964   *Caribou Eskimos of the Upper Kazan River, Keewatin*. The Allen Press, Kansas.

Heard, D. C.
    1981   *An Estimate of the Size and Structure of the Kaminuriak Caribou Herd In 1977*. Wildlife Service Government of the Northwest Territories, Ottawa.

Hearne, S.
    1958   *A Journey From Prince of Wales's Fort in Hudson's Bay to the Northern Ocean: 1769,1770,1771,1772*. The Macmillan Company of Canada LTD., Toronto.

Hedges, R. E. M. and A. R. Millard
    1995   Bones and Groundwater: Towards the Modelling of Diagenetic Processes. *Journal of Archaeological Science* 22:155-164.

Hedges, R. E. M. and A. R. Millard
    1995   Measurements and Relationships of Diagenetic Alteration of Bone from Three Archaeological Sites. *Journal of Archaeological Science* 22:201-209.

Henderson, L.
    1997   The Arvia'juaq and Qikitaaruk Oral History Project. In *At a Crossroads: Archaeology and First Peoples in Canada*, edited by G. Nicholas and T. Andrews. Simon Fraser University, Burnaby.

Hume, I. N.
    1969   *A Guide to Artifacts of Colonial America*. University of Pennsylvania Press, Phulidelphia.

Hunter, J. G.
    1968   Fishes and Fisheries. *In Scienc, History and Hudson Bay*, edited by C. S. Beals, pp. 360-377. vol. I. Department of Mines and Natural Resources, Ottawa.

Hunziker, O.
    1914   *Condensed Milk and Milk Powder*. Hunziker, LaFayette, Indiana.

Jenness, D.
    1922   *The Life of the Copper Eskimos. Report of the Canadian Arctic Expedition 1913-1918 12*. King's Printer, Ottawa.

Jones, R. F.
    1989   *The Keewatin Inuit and Interband Trade and Communications*, University of Manitoba.

Jones, O. R.
   2000   A Guide to Dating Glass Tableware: 1800 to 1940. In *Studies in Material Culture Research*, edited by K. Karklins, pp. 141-232. The Society for Historical Archaeology, California, Pennsylvania.

Judge, A.
   1914   *A History of the Canning Industry by its Most Prominent Men*. The Canning Trade, Baltimore.

Kalluak, M.
   1974   *How Kabloonat Became and other Inuit Stories*. Government of Northwest Territories, Yellowknife.

Karklins, K.
   1992   *Trade Ornament Usage Among Native Peoples of Canada - A Source Book*. Studies in Archaeology, Architecture, and History. National Historic Sites Parks Service, Environment Canada.

Keith, D.
   2004   Caribou, River and Ocean: Harvaqtuurmiut Landscape Organization and Orientation. *Inuit Studies* 28(2):39-56.

Kenney, J. F.
   1932   Historical Introduction and Notes. In *The Founding of Churchill; Being the Journal of Captain James Knight, Govenor-in-Chief in Hudson Bay*, edited by J. F. Kenney. J.M. Dent and Sons LTD., Toronto.

Kenyon, W. A.
   1985   *The History of James Bay 1610-1686*. Archaeology Monograph 10. Royal Ontario Museum, Toronto.

Knight, J.
   1932   *The Founding of Churchill: Being the Journal of Captain James Knight, Govenor-in-Chief in Hudson Bay from 14th July to 13th of September 1717*. J.M Dent & Sons, Toronto.

LeBlanc, R. J.
   1994   *The Crane Site and the Paleoeskimo Period in the Western Canadian Arctic*. Archaeological Survey of Canada Mercury Series 148. Canadian Museum of Civilization, Ottawa.

Leden, C.
   1990   *Across the Keewatin Icefields*. Translated by L. Neatby. Watson & Dwyer Publishing, Winnipeg.

Lee, M. and G. Reinhardt
   2003   *Eskimo Architecture: Dwelling and Structure in the Early Historic Period*. University of Alaska Press, Fairbanks.

Leone, M. P. and P. B. Potter
   1988   Introduction: Issues in Historical Archaeology. In *The Recovery of Meaning: Historical Archaeology in the Eastern United States*, edited by M. Leone and P. Potter. Smithsonian Institution Press, Washington D.C.

Linnamae, I. and B. L. Clark
   1976   Archaeology of Rankin Inlet, N.W.T. *Musk-Ox* 19:37-73.

Lunn, N. J., I. Stirling and S. N. Nowicki
   1997   Distribution and Abundance of Ringed (*Phoca hispida*) and Bearded (*Erignathus barbatus*) in Western Hudson Bay. *Canadian Journal of Fish and Aquatic Science* 54:914-941.

Lyman, R. L.
   1984   Bone Density and Differential Survivorship of Fossil Classes. *Journal of Anthropological Archaeology* 3:259-199.

   1985   Bone Frequencies: Differential Survivorship of Fossil Classes. *Journal of Archaeological Science* 12:221-236.

   1994   Quantitative Units and Terminology in Zooarchaeology. *American Antiquity* 59(1):36-71.

Lyman, R. L., J. M. Savelle and P. Whitridge
   1992   Derivation and Application of a Meat Utility Index for Phocid Seals. *Journal of Archaeological Science* 19:532-555.

Lyons, N.
   2007   *Natasha Lyons' Unpublished Field Notes from the 2007 Arviat Oral History Project*. University of Calgary.

Macpherson, A. H.
   1968   Land Mammals. In *Science, and History Hudson Bay*, edited by C. S. Beals, pp. 466-501. vol. 1. Department of Mines and Natural Resources, Ottawa.

Mansfield, A. W.
   1968   Seals and Walrus. In *Science, History, and Hudon Bay*, edited by C. S. Beals and D. A. Shenstone, pp. 378-387. vol. 1. Department of Enerfy, Mines, and Resources, Ottawa.

Mary-Rousselliere, G.
   1979   The Thule Culture on North Baffin Island: Early Thule Charachteristics and the Survival of the Thule Tradition. In *Thule Eskimo Culture: An Anthropological Restrospective*, edited by A. P. McCartney. vol. 88. Canadian Museum of Civilzation, Ottawa.

Mathiasson, T.
   1928   *Material Culture of the Iglulik Eskimos*. Report of the Fifth Thule Expedition 1921-24 6 No.1. Gyldendalske Boghandel Nordisk Forlag, Copenhagen.

McMartin, I. and L. A. Dredge
   2005   *History of Ice Flow in the Schultz Lake and Wager Bay Areas, Kivalliq Region, Nunavut*. Geologial Survey of Canada, Current Research. Department of Natural Resources, Ottawa.

Morlan, R. E.
   1994   Oxbow Bison Procurement as seen from the Harder Site, Saskatchewan. *Journal of Archaeological Science* 21:757-777.

Nash, R.
   1972   Pre-Dorset Culture in Northeastern Manitoba. *Arctic Anthropology* 9(1):10-16.

―

   1975   *Archaeological Investigations in the Transitional Forest Zone: Northern Manitoba, Southern Keewatin N.W.T.* Manitoba Museum of Man and Nature, Winnipeg.

Nelson, L. H.
   1963   Nail Chronology as an Aid to Dating Old Buildings. *History News* 19(2).

Nicholson, R. A.
   1996   Bone Degradations, Burial Medium, and Species Representation: Debunking the Myths, and Experiment-based Approach. *Journal of Archaeological Science* 23:513-533.

Oetelaar, G.
   1991   *Faunal Remains at Arviat - Appendix to Permit 89-663 (1989) Report*. Prince of Wales Northern Heritage Centre, Yellowknife.

Paine, F. A.
   1977   *The Packaging Media*. Blackie & Son Limited, Glasgow and London.

Parker, G. R.
   1972   *Distribution of Barren Ground Caribou Harvest in Northcentral Canada from Ear-Tag Returns*. Occasional Papers, Canada Wildlife Services, Ottawa.

Pilgram, T. and F. Marshall
   1995   Bone Counts and Statisticians: a Reply to Ringrose. Journal of Archaeological Science 22(93-97).

Post, L.
   2004   *Pinniped Projects: Articulating Seal and Sea Lion Skeletons*. Bone Building Books.

Rae, J.
   1866   On the Equimaux. *Transactions of the Ethnological Society of London* 4:138-153.

―

   1953   *Rae's Arctic Correspondence*. The Hudson's bay Record Society, London.

―

   1970   *Narrative of an Expedition to the Shores of the Arctic Sea in 1846 & 1847*. Canadiana House.

Rasmussen, K.
   1930   *Observations on the Intellectual Culture of the Caribou Eskimos. Report of the Fifth Thule Expedition 1921-24* 7 No. 2. Glydendalske Boghandel, Nordisk Forlag, Copenhagen.

Reitz, E. J. and E. S. Wing
   1999   *Zooarchaeology*. Cambridge Manuals in Archaeology. Cambridge University Press, Cambridge.

Rich, E. E. (editor)
   1953   *Rae's Arctic Correspondence*. The Hudson Bay Record Society 1844-1855, London.

Riewe, R.
   1991   Inuit Use of Sea Ice. *Arctic and Alpine Research* 23(1):3-10.

―

   1992   *Nunavut Atlas*. Canadian Circumplar Institute and Tungavik Federation of Nunavut, Edmonton.

Ringrose, T. J.
   1993   Bone Counts and Statistics: A Critique. *Journal of Archaeological Science* 20:121-157.

   1995   Repsonse to Pilgram and Marshall "Bone Counts and Statisticians: a Reply to Ringrose". *Journal of Archaeological Science* 22:99-102.

Ritchie, J. C.
   2004   *Post-Glacial Vegetation of Canada*. Cambridge University Press, Cambridge.

Robinson, J. L.
   1968   Geography of Hudson Bay. In *Science, History, and Hudson Bay*, edited by C. S. Beals. vol. I. Department of Energy, Mines, and Resources, Ottawa.

Robson, J.
   1759   *An Accont of 6 Years Residence in Hudson Bay: From 1733-36 & 1744-47*. J. Jeffreys, London.

Rogers, A. R.
   2000   Analysis of Bone Counts by Maximum Likelihood. *Journal of Archaeological Science* 27:111-125.

Ross, W. G.
   1975   *Whaling and Eskimos: Hudson Bay 1860-1915*. Mercury Series 10. National Museum of Man, Ottawa.

Ross, L. A. and J. D. Light
   2000   A Field Guide to the Description and Interpretation of Metal Files. In *Studies in Material Culture Research*, edited by K. Karklins, pp. 20-32. The Society for Historical Archaeology, California, Pennsylvania.

Sacharow, S. and R. C. Griffin
   1970   *Food Packaging: A Guide for the Supplier, Processor and Distributor*. AVI Publishing Co., Westport, Connecticut.

Savile, D. B. O.
   1968   Flora and Fauna of Land Areas. In *Science, History, and Hudson Bay*, edited by C. S. Beals. Department of Energy, Mines and Resources, Ottawa.

Smith, T. G.
   1975   Ringed Seals in James Bay and Hudson Bay: Population Estimates and Catch Statistics. *Arctic* 28(3):170-182.

Smith, J. G. E. and E. S. Burch
   1979   Chipewyan and Inuit in the Central Canadian Subarctic, 1613-1977. *Arctic Anthropology* 16(2):76-100.

Smith, T. G., M. O. Hammill and G. Taugbol
   1991   Review of the Developmental, Behavioural, and Physiological Adaptations of the Ringed Seal, Phoca Hispida, to Life in the Arctic Winter. *Arctic* 44(2):124-131.

Steenhoven, G.
   1955a   *Report to the Department of Northern Affairs and National Resources on a Field Research Journey for the Study of Legal Concepts Among the Eskimo in some Parts of the Keewatin District, In the Summer of 1955 - 1*. Department of Northern Affairs and National Resources, Ottawa.

   1955b   *Report to the Department of Northern Affairs and National Resources on a Field Research Journey for the Study of Legal Concepts Among the Eskimo in some Parts of the Keewatin District, In the Summer of 1955 - 2 Attachment II*. Department of Northern Affairs and National Resources, Ottawa.

   1955c   *Report to the Department of Northern Affairs and National Resources on a Field Research Journey for the Study of Legal Concepts Among the Eskimo in some Parts of the Keewatin District, In the Summer of 1955 - 3 Supplement*. Department of Northern Affairs and National Resources, Ottawa.

Stevenson, M.G.
   1997   *Inuit, Whalers, and Cultural Persistence*. Oxford University Press, Oxford.

Stewart, A. M.
   1994   *Caribou Inuit Settlement Response to Changing Resource Availability on the Kazan River, Northwest Territories, Canada*, Doctor of Philosophy, University of California.

Thompson, H. A.
   1968   The Climate of Hudson Bay. In *Science, History and Hudson Bay*, edited by C. S. Beals. vol. I. Department of Energy, Mines and Resources, Ottawa.

Thompson, D. C., G. H. Klassen and J. Cihlar
   1980   Caribou Habitat Mapping in the Southern District of Keewatin NWT: An Application of Digital Landsat Data. *Journal of Applied Ecology* 17:125-138.

Vallee, F. G.
  1967 *Kabloona and Eskimo in the Central Keewatin.* St. Paul University, Ottawa.

Van de Velde, O.
  1976 Seal Sharing Partnerships among the Pelly Bay Inuit. In *Inuit Land Use and Occupancy Project,* edited by M. Freeman, pp. 187-191. vol. 2. Department of Indian and Northern Affairs, Ottawa.

Wakelyn, L.
  1999 *The Qamanirjuaq Herd: An Arctic Enigma.* The Beverly and Qamanirjuaq Caribou Management Board, Iqaluit.

Wallerstein, I
  1974 *The Modem World-System, I.* Academic, New York.

  1980 *The Modem World-System, II.* Academic, New York.

Wells, T.
  1998 Nail Chronology: The Use of Technologically Derived Features. *Historical Archaeology* 32(3):78-99.

Whitridge, P.
  2001 Zen Fish: A Consideration of the Discordance between Artifactual and Zooarchaeological Indicators of Thule Fish Use. *Journal of Anthropological Archaeology* 20:3-72.

Williams, G. and R. Glover
  1969 Introduction. In *Andrew Graham's Observations on Hudson's Bay 1767-91,* edited by G. Williams and R. Glover, pp. xiii-lxxii. The Hudson's Bay Record Society, London.

Wright, J. V.
  1972 *The Shield Archaic.* Publications in Archaeology 3. National Museums of Canada, Ottawa.

  1976 *The Grant Lake Site, Keewatin District N.W.T.* Mercury Series 47. Archaeological Survey of Canada, Ottawa.

Wrigley, R. E.
  1974 Ecological Notes on Animals of the Churchill Region of Hudson Bay. *Arctic* 27(3):201-214.

Zoltai, S. C. and J. D. Johnson
  1978 *Vegetation-Soil Relationships in the Keewatin District.* Canadian Forestry Service, Ottawa.

www.ingramcontent.com/pod-product-compliance
Lightning Source LLC
Chambersburg PA
CBHW061549010526
44115CB00023B/2992